DECLAMATION ON THE
NOBILITY AND PREEMINENCE
OF THE FEMALE SEX

THE
OTHER VOICE
IN
EARLY MODERN
EUROPE

A series edited by
Margaret L. King and
Albert Rabil, Jr.

Henricus Cornelius Agrippa

DECLAMATION ON THE NOBILITY AND PREEMINENCE OF THE FEMALE SEX

*Translated and Edited
with an Introduction by
Albert Rabil, Jr.*

THE UNIVERSITY OF CHICAGO PRESS
Chicago and London

Albert Rabil, Jr., is distinguished teaching professor of humanities at the State University of New York, Old Westbury. His earlier books include *Merleau-Ponty: Existentialist of the Social World* (1967) and *Erasmus and the New Testament: The Mind of a Christian Humanist* (1972).

The University of Chicago Press, Chicago 60637
The University of Chicago Press, Ltd., London
© 1996 by The University of Chicago
All rights reserved. Published 1996
Printed in the United States of America
05 04 03 02 01 00 99 98   2 3 4 5

ISBN: 0-226-01058-9 (cloth)
ISBN: 0-226-01059-7 (paper)

Library of Congress Cataloging-in-Publication Data

Agrippa von Nettesheim, Heinrich Cornelius, 1486?–1535.
    [Declamatio de nobilitate et praecellentia foeminei sexus.
English]
    Declamation on the nobility and preeminence of the female sex /
Henricus Cornelius Agrippa : translated and edited with an
introduction by Albert Rabil, Jr.
        p.   cm. — (The other voice in early modern Europe)
    Includes bibliographical references.
    ISBN 0-226-01058-9 (cloth). — ISBN 0-226-01059-7 (pbk.)
    1. Women—Early works to 1800.   2. Feminism—Early works to 1800.
I. Rabil, Albert.   II. Title.   III. Series.
HQ1201.A3213   1993
305.4—dc20   96-3307
                                                         CIP

♾ The paper used in this publication meets the minimum requirements of
the American National Standard for Information Sciences—Permanence
of Paper for Printed Library Materials, ANSI Z39.48-1984.

To feminist colleagues of many years
whose strengths and courage in many contexts I have witnessed
and whose accomplishments I have admired.
Especially the following:

Patricia Barnes-McConnell

Minna Barrett

Anne Barstow

Eileen Bender

Sidney Bremer

Alice Carse
(1932–91)

Elizabeth Clark

Christine Downing

Janet Ray Edwards

Selby Hickey

Margaret L. King

Billie Maguire

Lauren Randel

Naomi Rosenthal

Merrill Skaggs

Rhea Whitehead

CONTENTS

EDITORS' INTRODUCTION
TO THE SERIES

THE OLD VOICE AND THE OTHER VOICE

In western Europe and the United States women are nearing equality in the professions, in business, and in politics. Most enjoy access to education, reproductive rights, and autonomy in financial affairs. Issues vital to women are on the public agenda: equal pay, child care, domestic abuse, breast cancer research, and curricular revision with an eye to the inclusion of women.

These recent achievements have their origins in things women (and some male supporters) said for the first time about six hundred years ago. Theirs is the "other voice," in contradistinction to the "first voice," the voice of the educated men who created western culture. Coincident with a general reshaping of European culture in the period 1300 to 1700 (called the Renaissance or Early Modern period), questions of female equality and opportunity were raised that still resound and are still unresolved.

The "other voice" emerged against the backdrop of a 3,000-year history of misogyny—the hatred of women—rooted in the civilizations related to western culture: Hebrew, Greek, Roman, and Christian. Misogyny inherited from these traditions pervaded the intellectual, medical, legal, religious and social systems that developed during the European Middle Ages.

The following pages describe the misogynistic tradition inherited by early modern Europeans, and the new tradition which the "other voice" called into being to challenge its assumptions. This review should serve as a framework for the understanding of the texts published in the series "The Other Voice in Early Modern Europe." Introductions specific to each text and author follow this essay in all the volumes of the series.

THE MISOGYNIST TRADITION, 500 BCE–1500 CE

Embedded in the philosophical and medical theories of the ancient Greeks were perceptions of the female as inferior to the male in both mind and body. Similarly, the structure of civil legislation inherited from the ancient Romans was biased against women, and the views on women developed by Christian thinkers out of the Hebrew Bible and the Christian New Testament were negative and disabling. Literary works composed in the vernacular language of ordinary people, and widely recited or read, conveyed these negative assumptions. The social networks within which most women lived—those of the family and the institutions of the Roman Catholic church—were shaped by this misogynist tradition and sharply limited the areas in which women might act in and upon the world.

GREEK PHILOSOPHY AND FEMALE NATURE   Greek biology assumed that women were inferior to men and defined them merely as child-bearers and housekeepers. This view was authoritatively expressed in the works of the philosopher Aristotle.

Aristotle thought in dualities. He considered action superior to inaction, form (the inner design or structure of any object) superior to matter, completion to incompletion, possession to deprivation. In each of these dualities, he associated the male principle with the superior quality and the female with the inferior. "The male principle in nature," he argued, "is associated with active, formative and perfected characteristics, while the female is passive, material and deprived, desiring the male in order to become complete."[1] Men are always identified with virile qualities, such as judgment, courage and stamina; women with their opposites—irrationality, cowardice, and weakness.

Even in the womb, the masculine principle was considered superior. Man's semen, Aristotle believed, created the form of a new human creature, while the female body contributed only matter. (The existence of the ovum, and the other facts of human embryology, were not established until the seventeenth century.) Although the later Greek physician Galen believed that there was a female component in generation, contributed by "female semen," the followers of both Aristotle and Galen saw the male role in human generation as more active and more important.

In the Aristotelian view, the male principle sought always to reproduce itself. The creation of a female was always a mistake, therefore, resulting

1. Aristotle, *Physics*, 1.9 192a20–24 (*The Complete Works of Aristotle*, ed. Jonathan Barnes, rev. Oxford translation, 2 vols. [Princeton, 1984], 1:328).

from an imperfect act of generation. Every female born was considered a "defective" or "mutilated" male (as Aristotle's terminology has variously been translated), a "monstrosity" of nature.[2]

For Greek theorists, the biology of males and females was the key to their psychology. The female was softer and more docile, more apt to be despondent, querulous, and deceitful. Being incomplete, moreover, she craved sexual fulfillment in intercourse with a male. The male was intellectual, active, and in control of his passions.

These psychological polarities derived from the theory that the universe consisted of four elements (earth, fire, air and water), expressed in human bodies as four "humors" (black bile, yellow bile, blood, and phlegm) considered respectively dry, hot, damp, and cold, and corresponding to mental states ("melancholic," "choleric," "sanguine," "phlegmatic"). In this schematization, the male, sharing the principles of earth and fire, was dry and hot; the female, sharing the principles of air and water, was cold and damp.

Female psychology was further affected by her dominant organ, the uterus (womb), *hystera* in Greek. The passions generated by the womb made women lustful, deceitful, talkative, irrational, indeed—when these affects were in excess—"hysterical."

Aristotle's biology also had social and political consequences. If the male principle was superior and the female inferior, then in the household, as in the state, men should rule and women must be subordinate. That hierarchy does not rule out the companionship of husband and wife, whose cooperation was necessary for the welfare of children and the preservation of property. Such mutuality supported male preeminence.

Aristotle's teacher Plato suggested a different possibility: that men and women might possess the same virtues. The setting for this proposal is the imaginary and ideal Republic that Plato sketches in a dialogue of that name. Here, for a privileged elite capable of leading wisely, all distinctions of class and wealth dissolve, as do consequently those of gender. Without households or property, as Plato constructs his ideal society, there is no need for the subordination of women. Women may, therefore, be educated to the same level as men to assume leadership responsibilities. Plato's Republic remained imaginary, however. In real societies, the subordination of women remained the norm and the prescription.

The views of women inherited from the Greek philosophical tradition became the basis for medieval thought. In the thirteenth century, the

2. Aristotle, *Generation of Animals*, 2.3 737a27–28 (Barnes, 1:1144).

supreme scholastic philosopher Thomas Aquinas, among others, still echoed Aristotle's views of human reproduction, of male and female personalities, and of the preeminent male role in the social hierarchy.

ROMAN LAW AND THE FEMALE CONDITION Roman law, like Greek philosophy, underlay medieval thought and shaped medieval society. The ancient belief that adult, property-owning men should administer households and make decisions affecting the community at large is the very fulcrum of Roman law.

Around 450 BCE, during Rome's republican era, the community's customary law was recorded (legendarily) on Twelve Tables erected in the city's central forum. It was later elaborated by professional jurists whose activity increased in the imperial era, when much new legislation, especially on issues affecting family and inheritance, was passed. This growing, changing body of laws was eventually codified in the *Corpus of Civil Law* under the direction of the Emperor Justinian, generations after the empire ceased to be ruled from Rome. That *Corpus*, read and commented upon by medieval scholars from the eleventh century on, inspired the legal systems of most of the cities and kingdoms of Europe.

Laws regarding dowries, divorce, and inheritance most pertain to women. Since those laws aimed to maintain and preserve property, the women concerned were those from the property-owning minority. Their subordination to male family members points to the even greater subordination of lower-class and slave women about whom the laws speak little.

In the early Republic, the *paterfamilias*, "father of the family," possessed *patria potestas*, "paternal power." The term *pater*, "father," in both these cases does not necessarily mean biological father, but householder. The father was the person who owned the household's property and, indeed, its human members. The *paterfamilias* had absolute power—including the power, rarely exercised, of life or death—over his wife, his children, and his slaves, as much as over his cattle.

Children could be "emancipated," an act that granted legal autonomy and the right to own property. Male children over the age of fourteen could be emancipated by a special grant from the father, or automatically by their father's death. But females never could be emancipated; instead, they passed from the authority of their father to a husband or, if widowed or orphaned while still unmarried, to a guardian or tutor.

Marriage under its traditional form placed the woman under her husband's authority, or *manus*. He could divorce her on grounds of adultery, drinking wine, or stealing from the household, but she could not divorce him. She could possess no property in her own right, nor bequeath any to her children upon her death. When her husband died, the household property passed not to her but to his male heirs. And when her father died, she had no claim to any family inheritance, which was directed to her brothers or more remote male relatives. The effect of these laws was to exclude women from civil society, itself based on property ownership.

In the later Republican and Imperial periods, these rules were significantly modified. Women rarely married according to the traditional form, but according to the form of "free" marriage. That practice allowed a woman to remain under her father's authority, to possess property given her by her father (most frequently the "dowry," recoverable from the husband's household in the event of his death), and to inherit from her father. She could also bequeath property to her own children and divorce her husband, just as he could divorce her.

Despite this greater freedom, women still suffered enormous disability under Roman law. Heirs could belong only to the father's side, never the mother's. Moreover, although she could bequeath her property to her children, she could not establish a line of succession in doing so. A woman was "the beginning and end of her own family," growled the jurist Ulpian. Moreover, women could play no public role. They could not hold public office, represent anyone in a legal case, or even witness a will. Women had only a private existence, and no public personality.

The dowry system, the guardian, women's limited ability to transmit wealth, and total political disability are all features of Roman law adopted, although modified according to local customary laws, by the medieval communities of western Europe.

CHRISTIAN DOCTRINE AND WOMEN'S PLACE The Hebrew Bible and the Christian New Testament authorized later writers to limit women to the realm of the family and to burden them with the guilt of original sin. The passages most fruitful for this purpose were the creation narratives in Genesis and sentences from the Epistles defining women's role within the Christian family and community.

Each of the first two chapters of Genesis contains a creation narrative. In the first "God created man in his own image, in the image of God he created him; male and female he created them." (NRSV, Genesis 1:27) In the second, God created Eve from Adam's rib (2:21–23). Christian theologians relied principally on Genesis 2 for their understanding of the relation between man and woman, interpreting the creation of Eve from Adam as proof of her subordination to him.

The creation story in Genesis 2 leads to that of the temptations in Genesis 3: of Eve by the wily serpent, and of Adam by Eve. As read by Christian theologians from Tertullian to Thomas Aquinas, the narrative made Eve responsible for the Fall and its consequences. She instigated the act; she deceived her husband; she suffered the greater punishment. Her disobedience made it necessary for Jesus to be incarnated and to die on the cross. From the pulpit, moralists and preachers for centuries conveyed to women the guilt that they bore for original sin.

The Epistles offered advice to early Christians on building communities of the faithful. Among the matters to be regulated was the place of women. Paul offered views favorable to women in Galatians 3:28: "There is neither Jew nor Greek, there is neither slave nor free, there is neither male nor female; for you are all one in Christ Jesus." Paul also referred to women as his co-workers and placed them on a par with himself and his male co-workers (Phil. 4:2–3; Rom. 16:1–3; I Cor. 16:19). Elsewhere Paul limited women's possibilities: "But I want you to understand that the head of every man is Christ, the head of a woman is her husband, and the head of Christ is God." (I Cor. 11:3)

Biblical passages by later writers (though attributed to Paul) enjoined women to forego jewels, expensive clothes, and elaborate coiffures; and they forbade women to "teach or have authority over men," telling them to "learn in silence with all submissiveness" as is proper for one responsible for sin, consoling them however with the thought that they will be saved through childbearing (I Tim. 2:9–15). Other texts among the later epistles defined women as the weaker sex, and emphasized their subordination to their husbands (I Peter 3:7; Col. 3:18; Eph. 5:22–23).

These passages from the New Testament became the arsenal employed by theologians of the early church to transmit negative attitudes toward women to medieval Christian culture—above all, Tertullian ("On the Apparel of Women"), Jerome (*Against Jovinian*), and Augustine (*The Literal Meaning of Genesis*).

THE IMAGE OF WOMEN IN MEDIEVAL LITERATURE The philosophical, legal and religious traditions born in antiquity formed the basis of the medieval intellectual synthesis wrought by trained thinkers, mostly clerics, writing in Latin and based largely in universities. The vernacular literary tradition which developed alongside the learned tradition also spoke about female nature and women's roles. Medieval stories, poems, and epics were also infused with misogyny. They portrayed most women as lustful and deceitful, while praising good housekeepers and loyal wives, or replicas of the Virgin Mary, or the female saints and martyrs.

There is an exception in the movement of "courtly love" that evolved in southern France from the twelfth century. Courtly love was the erotic love between a nobleman and noblewoman, the latter usually superior in social rank. It was always adulterous. From the conventions of courtly love derive modern western notions of romantic love. The phenomenon has had an impact disproportionate to its size, for it affected only a tiny elite, and very few women. The exaltation of the female lover probably does not reflect a higher evaluation of women, or a step toward their sexual liberation. More likely it gives expression to the social and sexual tensions besetting the knightly class at a specific historical juncture.

The literary fashion of courtly love was on the wane by the thirteenth century, when the widely read *Romance of the Rose* was composed in French by two authors of significantly different dispositions. Guillaume de Lorris composed the initial 4,000 verses around 1235, and Jean de Meun added about 17,000 verses—more than four times the original—around 1265.

The fragment composed by Guillaume de Lorris stands squarely in the courtly love tradition. Here the poet, in a dream, is admitted into a walled garden where he finds a magic fountain in which a rosebush is reflected. He longs to pick one rose but the thorns around it prevent his doing so, even as he is wounded by arrows from the God of Love, whose commands he agrees to obey. The remainder of this part of the poem recounts the poet's unsuccessful efforts to pluck the rose.

The longer part of the *Romance* by Jean de Meun also describes a dream. But here allegorical characters give long didactic speeches, providing a social satire on a variety of themes, including those pertaining to women. Love is an anxious and tormented state, the poem explains, women are greedy and manipulative, marriage is miserable, beautiful women are lustful, ugly ones cease to please, and a chaste woman, as rare as a black swan, can scarcely be found.

Shortly after Jean de Meun completed *The Romance of the Rose*, Mathéolus penned his *Lamentations*, a long Latin diatribe against marriage translated into French about a century later. The *Lamentations* sum up medieval attitudes toward women and provoked the important response by Christine de Pizan in her *Book of the City of Ladies*.

In 1355, Giovanni Boccaccio wrote *Il Corbaccio*, another antifeminist manifesto, though ironically by an author whose other works pioneered new directions in Renaissance thought. The former husband of his lover appears to Boccaccio, condemning his unmoderated lust and detailing the defects of women. Boccaccio concedes at the end "how much men naturally surpass women in nobility"[3] and is cured of his desires.

---

3. Giovanni Boccaccio, *The Corbaccio or The Labyrinth of Love*, trans. and ed. Anthony K. Cassell (Binghamton, N.Y., rev. paper ed., 1993), 71.

WOMEN'S ROLES: THE FAMILY The negative perception of women expressed in the intellectual tradition are also implicit in the actual roles that women played in European society. Assigned to subordinate positions in the household and the church, they were barred from significant participation in public life.

Medieval European households, like those in antiquity and in non-western civilizations, were headed by males. It was the male serf, or peasant, feudal lord, town merchant, or citizen who was polled or taxed or succeeded to an inheritance or had any acknowledged public role, although their wives or widows could stand on a temporary basis as surrogates for them. From about 1100, the position of property-holding males was enhanced further. Inheritance was confined to the male, or agnate, line—with depressing consequences for women.

A wife never fully belonged to her husband's family or a daughter to her father's family. She left her father's house young to marry whomever her parents chose. Her dowry was managed by her husband and normally passed to her children by him at her death.

A married woman's life was occupied nearly constantly with cycles of pregnancy, childbearing, and lactation. Women bore children through all the years of their fertility, and many died in childbirth before the end of that term. They also bore responsibility for raising young children up to six or seven. That responsibility was shared in the propertied classes, since it was common for a wet-nurse to take over the job of breastfeeding, and servants took over other chores.

Women trained their daughters in the household responsibilities appropriate to their status, nearly always in tasks associated with textiles: spinning, weaving, sewing, embroidering. Their sons were sent out of the house as apprentices or students, or their training was assumed by fathers in later childhood and adolescence. On the death of her husband, a woman's children became the responsibility of his family. She generally did not take "his" children with her to a new marriage or back to her father's house, except sometimes in artisan classes.

Women also worked. Rural peasants performed farm chores, merchant wives often practiced their husband's trade, the unmarried daughters of the urban poor worked as servants or prostitutes. All wives produced or embellished textiles and did the housekeeping, while wealthy ones managed servants. These labors were unpaid or poorly paid, but often contributed substantially to family wealth.

WOMEN'S ROLES: THE CHURCH Membership in a household, whether a father's or a husband's, meant for women a lifelong subordination to others.

In western Europe, the Roman Catholic church offered an alternative to the career of wife and mother. A woman could enter a convent parallel in function to the monasteries for men that evolved in the early Christian centuries.

In the convent, a woman pledged herself to a celibate life, lived according to strict community rules, and worshipped daily. Often the convent offered training in Latin, allowing some women to become considerable scholars and authors, as well as scribes, artists, and musicians. For women who chose the conventual life, the benefits could be enormous, but for numerous others placed in convents by paternal choice, the life could be restrictive and burdensome.

The conventual life declined as an alternative for women as the modern age approached. Reformed monastic institutions resisted responsibility for related female orders. The church increasingly restricted female institutional life by insisting on closer male supervision.

Women often sought other options. Some joined the communities of laywomen that sprang up spontaneously in the thirteenth century in the urban zones of western Europe, especially in Flanders and Italy. Some joined the heretical movements that flourished in late medieval Christendom, whose anticlerical and often antifamily positions particularly appealed to women. In these communities, some women were acclaimed as "holy women" or "saints," while others often were condemned as frauds or heretics.

In all, though the options offered to women by the church were sometimes less than satisfactory, sometimes they were richly rewarding. After 1520, the convent remained an option only in Roman Catholic territories. Protestantism engendered an ideal of marriage as a heroic endeavor, and appeared to place husband and wife on a more equal footing. Sermons and treatises, however, still called for female subordination and obedience.

THE OTHER VOICE, 1300–1700

Misogyny was so long-established in European culture when the modern era opened that to dismantle it was a monumental labor. The process began as part of a larger cultural movement that entailed the critical reexamination of ideas inherited from the ancient and medieval past. The humanists launched that critical reexamination.

THE HUMANIST FOUNDATION Originating in Italy in the fourteenth century, humanism quickly became the dominant intellectual movement in Europe. Spreading in the sixteenth century from Italy to the rest of Europe, it fueled the literary, scientific and philosophical movements of the era, and laid the basis for the eighteenth-century Enlightenment.

Humanists regarded the scholastic philosophy of medieval universities as out of touch with the realities of urban life. They found in the rhetorical discourse of classical Rome a language adapted to civic life and public speech. They learned to read, speak, and write classical Latin, and eventually classical Greek. They founded schools to teach others to do so, establishing the pattern for elementary and secondary education for the next three hundred years.

In the service of complex government bureaucracies, humanists employed their skills to write eloquent letters, deliver public orations, and formulate public policy. They developed new scripts for copying manuscripts and used the new printing press for the dissemination of texts, for which they created methods of critical editing.

Humanism was a movement led by males who accepted the evaluation of women in ancient texts and generally shared the misogynist perceptions of their culture. (Female humanists, as will be seen, did not.) Yet humanism also opened the door to the critique of the misogynist tradition. By calling authors, texts, and ideas into question, it made possible the fundamental re-reading of the whole intellectual tradition that was required in order to free women from cultural prejudice and social subordination.

A DIFFERENT CITY   The other voice first appeared when, after so many centuries, the accumulation of misogynist concepts evoked a response from a capable woman female defender: Christine de Pizan. Introducing her *Book of the City of Ladies* (1405), she described how she was affected by reading Mathéolus's *Lamentations*: "Just the sight of this book . . . made me wonder how it happened that so many different men . . . are so inclined to express both in speaking and in their treatises and writings so many wicked insults about women and their behavior."[4] These statements impelled her to detest herself "and the entire feminine sex, as though we were monstrosities in nature."[5]

The remainder of the *Book of the City of Ladies* presents a justification of the female sex and a vision of an ideal community of women. A pioneer, she has not only received the misogynist message, but she rejects it. From the fourteenth to seventeenth century, a huge body of literature accumulated that responded to the dominant tradition.

The result was a literary explosion consisting of works by both men and women, in Latin and in vernacular languages: works enumerating the achieve-

---

4. Christine de Pizan, *The Book of the City of Ladies*, trans. Earl Jeffrey Richards; Foreword Marina Warner (New York, 1982), I.1.1., pp. 3–4.

5. Ibid., I.1.1–2, p. 5.

ments of notable women; works rebutting the main accusations made against women; works arguing for the equal education of men and women; works defining and redefining women's proper role in the family, at court, and in public; and describing women's lives and experiences. Recent monographs and articles have begun to hint at the great range of this phenomenon, involving probably several thousand titles. The protofeminism of these "other voices" constitute a significant fraction of the literary product of the early modern era.

THE CATALOGUES Around 1365, the same Boccaccio whose *Corbaccio* rehearses the usual charges against female nature, wrote another work, *Concerning Famous Women*. A humanist treatise drawing on classical texts, it praised 106 notable women—one hundred of them from pagan Greek and Roman antiquity, and six from the religious and cultural tradition since antiquity—and helped make all readers aware of a sex normally condemned or forgotten. Boccaccio's outlook, nevertheless, is misogynist, for it singled out for praise those women who possessed the traditional virtues of chastity, silence, and obedience. Women who were active in the public realm, for example, rulers and warriors, were depicted as suffering terrible punishments for entering into the masculine sphere. Women were his subject, but Boccaccio's standard remained male.

Christine de Pizan's *Book of the City of Ladies* contains a second catalogue, one responding specifically to Boccaccio's. Where Boccaccio portrays female virtue as exceptional, she depicts it as universal. Many women in history were leaders, or remained chaste despite the lascivious approaches of men, or were visionaries and brave martyrs.

The work of Boccaccio inspired a series of catalogues of illustrious women of the biblical, classical, Christian, and local past: works by Alvaro de Luna, Jacopo Filippo Foresti (1497), Brantôme, Pierre Le Moyne, Pietro Paolo de Ribera (who listed 845 figures), and many others. Whatever their embedded prejudices, these catalogues of illustrious women drove home to the public the possibility of female excellence.

THE DEBATE At the same time, many questions remained: Could a woman be virtuous? Could she perform noteworthy deeds? Was she even, strictly speaking, of the same human species as men? These questions were debated over four centuries, in French, German, Italian, Spanish and English, by authors male and female, among Catholics, Protestants and Jews, in ponderous volumes and breezy pamphlets. The whole literary phenomenon has been called the *querelle des femmes*, the "Woman Question."

The opening volley of this battle occurred in the first years of the fifteenth century, in a literary debate sparked by Christine de Pizan. She exchanged letters critical of Jean de Meun's contribution to the *Romance of the Rose* with two French humanists and royal secretaries, Jean de Montreuil and Gontier Col. When the matter became public, Jean Gerson, one of Europe's leading theologians, supported de Pizan's arguments against de Meun, for the moment silencing the opposition.

The debate resurfaced repeatedly over the next two hundred years. *The Triumph of Women* (1438) by Juan Rodríguez de la Camara (or Juan Rodríguez del Padron) struck a new note by presenting arguments for the superiority of women to men. *The Champion of Women* (1440–42) by Martin Le Franc addresses once again the misogynist claims of *The Romance of the Rose*, and offers counterevidence of female virtue and achievement.

A cameo of the debate on women is included in the *Courtier*, one of the most-read books of the era, published by the Italian Baldassare Castiglione in 1528 and immediately translated into other European vernaculars. The *Courtier* depicts a series of evenings at the court of the Duke of Urbino in which many men and some women of the highest social stratum amuse themselves by discussing a range of literary and social issues. The "woman question" is a pervasive theme throughout, and the third of its four books is devoted entirely to that issue.

In a verbal duel, Gasparo Pallavicino and Giuliano de' Medici present the main claims of the two traditions—the prevailing misogynist one, and the newly emerging alternative one. Gasparo argues the innate inferiority of women and their inclination to vice. Only in bearing children do they profit the world. Giuliano counters that women share the same spiritual and mental capacities as men and may excel in wisdom and action. Men and women are of the same essence: just as no stone can be more perfectly a stone than another, so no human being can be more perfectly human than others, whether male or female. It was an astonishing assertion, boldly made to an audience as large as all Europe.

THE TREATISES Humanism provided the materials for a positive counterconcept to the misogyny embedded in scholastic philosophy and law, and inherited from the Greek, Roman and Christian pasts. A series of humanist treatises on marriage and family, education and deportment, and on the nature of women helped construct these new perspectives.

The works by Francesco Barbaro and Leon Battista Alberti, respectively *On Marriage* (1415) and *On the Family* (1434–37), far from defending female equality, reasserted women's responsibilities for rearing children and managing the housekeeping while being obedient, chaste, and silent. Nevertheless, they served the cause of reexamining the issue of women's nature by placing domestic issues at the center of scholarly concern and reopening the perti-

nent classical texts. In addition, Barbaro emphasized the companionate nature of marriage and the importance of a wife's spiritual and mental qualities
for the well-being of the family.

These themes reappear in later humanist works on marriage and the education of women by Juan Luis Vives and Erasmus. Both were moderately
sympathetic to the condition of women, without reaching beyond the usual
masculine prescriptions for female behavior.

An outlook more favorable to women characterizes the nearly unknown
work *In Praise of Women* (ca. 1487) by the Italian humanist Bartolommeo Goggio. In addition to providing a catalogue of illustrious women, Goggio
argued that male and female are the same in essence, but that women (re-
working from quite a new angle the Adam and Eve narrative) are actually
superior. In the same vein, the Italian humanist Maria Equicola asserted the
spiritual equality of men and women in *On Women* (1501). In 1525, Galeazzo
Flavio Capra (or Capella) published his work *On the Excellence and Dignity of
Women*. This humanist tradition of treatises defending the worthiness of
women culminates in the work of Henricus Cornelius Agrippa *On the Nobility
and Preeminence of the Female Sex*. No work by a male humanist more succinctly
or explicitly presents the case for female dignity.

THE WITCH BOOKS While humanists grappled with the issues pertaining to women and family, other learned men turned their attention to
what they perceived as a very great problem: witches. Witch-hunting man-
uals, explorations of the witch phenomenon, and even defenses of witches
are not at first glance pertinent to the tradition of the other voice. But they do
relate in this way: most accused witches were women. The hostility aroused
by supposed witch activity is comparable to the hostility aroused by women.
The evil deeds the victims of the hunt were charged with were exaggerations
of the vices to which, many believed, all women were prone.

The connection between the witch accusation and the hatred of women
is explicit in the notorious witch-hunting manual, *The Hammer of Witches*
(1486), by two Dominican inquisitors, Heinrich Krämer and Jacob Sprenger.
Here the inconstancy, deceitfulness, and lustfulness traditionally associated
with women are depicted in exaggerated form as the core features of witch
behavior. These inclined women to make a bargain with the devil—sealed
by sexual intercourse—by which they acquired unholy powers. Such bizarre
claims, far from being rejected by rational men, were broadcast by intellectuals. The German Ulrich Molitur, the Frenchman Nicolas Rémy, the Italian
Stefano Guazzo coolly informed the public of sinister orgies and midnight
pacts with the devil. The celebrated French jurist, historian and political
philosopher Jean Bodin argued that, because women were especially prone

to diabolism, regular legal procedures could properly be suspended in order to try those accused of this "exceptional crime."

A few experts, such as the physician Johann Weyer, a student of Agrippa's, raised their voices in protest. In 1563, he explained the witch phenomenon thus, without discarding belief in diabolism: the devil deluded foolish old women afflicted by melancholia, causing them to believe that they had magical powers. Weyer's rational skepticism, which had good credibility in the community of the learned, worked to revise the conventional views of women and witchcraft.

WOMEN'S WORKS To the many categories of works produced on the question of women's worth must be added nearly all works written by women. A woman writing was in herself a statement of women's claim to dignity.

Only a few women wrote anything prior to the dawn of the modern era, for three reasons. First, they rarely received the education that would enable them to write. Second, they were not admitted to the public roles—as administrator, bureaucrat, lawyer or notary, university professor—in which they might gain knowledge of the kinds of things the literate public thought worth writing about. Third, the culture imposed silence upon women, considering speaking out a form of unchastity. Given these conditions, it is remarkable that any women wrote. Those who did before the fourteenth century were almost always nuns or religious women whose isolation made their pronouncements more acceptable.

From the fourteenth century on, the volume of women's writings crescendoed. Women continued to write devotional literature, although not always as cloistered nuns. They also wrote diaries, often intended as keepsakes for their children; books of advice to their sons and daughters; letters to family members and friends; and family memoirs, in a few cases elaborate enough to be considered histories.

A few women wrote works directly concerning the "woman question," and some of these, such as the humanists Isotta Nogarola, Cassandra Fedele, Laura Cereta, and Olimpia Morata, were highly trained. A few were professional writers, living by the income of their pen: the very first among them Christine de Pizan, noteworthy in this context as in so many others. In addition to *The Book of the City of Ladies* and her critiques of *The Romance of the Rose*, she wrote *The Treasure of the City of Ladies* (a guide to social decorum for women), an advice book for her son, much courtly verse, and a full-scale history of the reign of king Charles V of France.

WOMEN PATRONS Women who did not themselves write but encouraged others to do so boosted the development of an alternative tradition.

Highly placed women patrons supported authors, artists, musicians, poets, and learned men. Such patrons, drawn mostly from the Italian elites and the courts of northern Europe, figure disproportionately as the dedicatees of the important works of early feminism.

For a start, it might be noted that the catalogues of Boccaccio and Alvaro de Luna were dedicated to the Florentine noblewoman Andrea Acciaiuoli and to Doña María, first wife of King Juan II of Castile, while the French translation of Boccaccio's work was commissioned by Anne of Brittany, wife of King Charles VIII of France. The humanist treatises of Goggio, Equicola, Vives, and Agrippa were dedicated, respectively, to Eleanora of Aragon, wife of Ercole I d'Este, duke of Ferrara; to Margherita Cantelma of Mantua; to Catherine of Aragon, wife of King Henry VIII of England; and to Margaret, duchess of Austria and regent of the Netherlands. As late as 1696, Mary Astell's *Serious Proposal to the Ladies, for the Advancement of Their True and Greatest Interest* was dedicated to Princess Ann of Denmark.

These authors presumed that their efforts would be welcome to female patrons, or they may have written at the bidding of those patrons. Silent themselves, perhaps even unresponsive, these loftily placed women helped shape the tradition of the other voice.

THE ISSUES The literary forms and patterns in which the tradition of the other voice presented itself have now been sketched. It remains to highlight the major issues about which this tradition crystallizes. In brief, there are four problems to which our authors return again and again, in plays and catalogues, in verse and in letters, in treatises and dialogues, in every language: the problem of chastity; the problem of power; the problem of speech; and the problem of knowledge. Of these the greatest, preconditioning the others, is the problem of chastity.

THE PROBLEM OF CHASTITY In traditional European culture, as in those of antiquity and others around the globe, chastity was perceived as woman's quintessential virtue—in contrast to courage, or generosity, or leadership, or rationality, seen as virtues characteristic of men. Opponents of women charged them with insatiable lust. Women themselves and their defenders—without disputing the validity of the standard—responded that women were capable of chastity.

The requirement of chastity kept women at home, silenced them, isolated them, left them in ignorance. It was the source of all other impediments. Why was it so important to the society of men, of whom chastity was not required, and who, more often than not, considered it their right to violate the chastity of any woman they encountered?

Female chastity ensured the continuity of the male-headed household. If a man's wife was not chaste, he could not be sure of the legitimacy of his offspring. If they were not his, and they acquired his property, it was not his household, but some other man's, that had endured. If his daughter was not chaste, she could not be transferred to another man's household as his wife, and he was dishonored.

The whole system of the integrity of the household and the transmission of property was bound up in female chastity. Such a requirement only pertained to property-owning classes, of course. Poor women could not expect to maintain their chastity, least of all if they were in contact with high-status men to whom all women but those of their own household were prey.

In Catholic Europe, the requirement of chastity was further buttressed by moral and religious imperatives. Original sin was inextricably linked with the sexual act. Virginity was seen as heroic virtue, far more impressive than, say, the avoidance of idleness or greed. Monasticism, the cultural institution that dominated medieval Europe for centuries, was grounded in the renunciation of the flesh. The Catholic reform of the eleventh century imposed a similar standard on all the clergy, and a heightened awareness of sexual requirements on all the laity. Although men were asked to be chaste, female unchastity was much worse: it led to the devil, as Eve had led mankind to sin.

To such requirements, women and their defenders protested their innocence. More, following the example of holy women who had escaped the requirements of family and sought the religious life, some women began to conceive of female communities as alternatives both to family and to the cloister. Christine de Pizan's city of ladies was such a community. Moderata Fonte and Mary Astell envisioned others. The luxurious salons of the French *précieuses* of the seventeenth century, or the comfortable English drawing rooms of the next, may have been born of the same impulse. Here women might not only escape, if briefly, the subordinate position that life in the family entailed, but they might make claims to power, exercise their capacity for speech, and display their knowledge.

THE PROBLEM OF POWER Women were excluded from power: the whole cultural tradition insisted upon it. Only men were citizens, only men bore arms, only men could be chiefs or lords or kings. There were exceptions which did not disprove the rule, when wives or widows or mothers took the place of men, awaiting their return or the maturation of a male heir. A woman who attempted to rule in her own right was perceived as an anomaly, a monster, at once a deformed woman and an insufficient male, sexually confused and, consequently, unsafe.

The association of such images with women who held or sought power explains some otherwise odd features of early modern culture. Queen Elizabeth I of England, one of the few women to hold full regal authority in European history, played with such male/female images—positive ones, of course—in representing herself to her subjects. She was a prince, and manly, even though she was female. She was also (she claimed) virginal, a condition absolutely essential if she was to avoid the attacks of her opponents. Catherine de' Medici, who ruled France as widow and regent for her sons, also adopted such imagery in defining her position. She chose as one symbol the figure of Artemisia, an androgynous ancient warrior-heroine, who combined a female persona with masculine powers.

Power in a woman, without such sexual imagery, seems to have been indigestible by the culture. A rare note was struck by the Englishman Sir Thomas Elyot in his *Defence of Good Women* (1540), justifying both women's participation in civic life and prowess in arms. The old tune was sung by the Scots reformer John Knox in his *First Blast of the Trumpet against the Monstrous Regiment of Women* (1558), for whom rule by women, defective in nature, was a hideous contradiction in terms.

The confused sexuality of the imagery of female potency was not reserved for rulers. Any woman who excelled was likely to be called an Amazon, recalling the self-mutilated warrior women of antiquity who repudiated all men, gave up their sons, and raised only their daughters. She was often said to have "exceeded her sex," or to have possessed "masculine virtue"—as the very fact of conspicuous excellence conferred masculinity, even on the female subject. The catalogues of notable women often showed those female heroes dressed in armor, armed to the teeth, like men. Amazonian heroines romp through the epics of the age—Ariosto's *Orlando Furioso* (1532), Spenser's *Faerie Queene* (1590–1609). Excellence in a woman was perceived as a claim for power, and power was reserved for the masculine realm. A woman who possessed either was masculinized, and lost title to her own female identity.

THE PROBLEM OF SPEECH Just as power had a sexual dimension when it was claimed by women, so did speech. A good woman spoke little. Excessive speech was an indication of unchastity. By speech, women seduced men. Eve had lured Adam into sin by her speech. Accused witches were commonly accused of having spoken abusively, or irrationally, or simply too much. As enlightened a figure as Francesco Barbaro insisted on silence in a woman, which he linked to her perfect unanimity with her husband's will and her unblemished virtue (her chastity). Another Italian humanist, Leonardo Bruni, in advising a noblewoman on her studies, barred her not from speech, but from public speaking. That was reserved for men.

Related to the problem of speech was that of costume, another, if silent, form of self-expression. Assigned the task of pleasing men as their primary occupation, elite women often tended to elaborate costume, hairdressing, and the use of cosmetics. Clergy and secular moralists alike condemned these practices. The appropriate function of costume and adornment was to announce the status of a woman's husband or father. Any further indulgence in adornment was akin to unchastity.

THE PROBLEM OF KNOWLEDGE When the Italian noblewoman Isotta Nogarola had begun to attain a reputation as a humanist, she was accused of incest—a telling instance of the association of learning in women with unchastity. That chilling association inclined any woman who was educated to deny that she was, or to make exaggerated claims of heroic chastity.

If educated women were pursued with suspicions of sexual misconduct, women seeking an education faced an even more daunting obstacle: the assumption that women were by nature incapable of learning, that reason was a particularly masculine ability. Just as they proclaimed their chastity, women and their defenders insisted upon their capacity for learning. The major work by a male writer on female education—*On the Education of a Christian Woman*, by Juan Luis Vives (1523)—granted female capacity for intellection, but argued still that a woman's whole education was to be shaped around the requirement of chastity and a future within the household. Female writers of the next generations—Marie de Gournay in France, Anna Maria van Schurman in Holland, Mary Astell in England—began to envision other possibilities.

The pioneers of female education were the Italian women humanists who managed to attain a Latin literacy and knowledge of classical and Christian literature equivalent to that of prominent men. Their works implicitly and explicitly raise questions about women's social roles, defining problems that beset women attempting to break out of the cultural limits that had bound them. Like Christine de Pizan, who achieved an advanced education through her father's tutoring and her own devices, their bold questioning makes clear the importance of training. Only when women were educated to the same standard as male leaders would they be able to raise that other voice and insist on their dignity as human beings morally, intellectually, and legally equal to men.

THE OTHER VOICE The other voice, a voice of protest, was mostly female, but also male. It spoke in the vernaculars and in Latin, in treatises and dialogues, plays and poetry, letters and diaries and pamphlets. It battered at the wall of misogynist beliefs that encircled women and raised a banner announcing its claims. The female was equal (or even superior) to the male in essential nature—moral, spiritual, intellectual. Women were capable of

essential nature—moral, spiritual, intellectual. Women were capable of higher education, of holding positions of power and influence in the public realm, and of speaking and writing persuasively. The last bastion of masculine supremacy, centered on the notions of a woman's primary domestic responsibility and the requirement of female chastity, was not as yet assaulted—although visions of productive female communities as alternatives to the family indicated an awareness of the problem.

During the period 1300 to 1700, the other voice remained only a voice, and one only dimly heard. It did not result—yet—in an alteration of social patterns. Indeed, to this day, they have not entirely been altered. Yet the call for justice issued as long as six centuries ago by those writing in the tradition of the other voice must be recognized as the source and origin of the mature feminist tradition and of the realignment of social institutions accomplished in the modern age.

We would like to thank the volume editors in this series, who responded with many suggestions to an earlier draft of this introduction, making it a collaborative enterprise. Many of their suggestions and criticisms have resulted in revisions of this introduction, though we remain responsible for the final product.

PROJECTED TITLES IN THE SERIES

Henricus Cornelius Agrippa, *Declamation on the Nobility and Preeminence of the Female Sex*, translated and edited by Albert Rabil, Jr.

Tullia d'Aragona, *Dialogue on the Infinity of Love*, edited and translated by Rinaldina Russell and Bruce Merry

Laura Cereta, *Collected Letters of a Renaissance Feminist*, edited and translated by Diana Robin

Cassandra Fedele, *Letters and Orations*, edited and translated by Diana Robin

Cecilia Ferrazzi, *Autobiography of an Aspiring Saint*, transcribed, translated, and annotated by Anne Jacobson Schutte

Moderata Fonte, *The Worth of Women*, edited and translated by Virginia Cox

Veronica Franco, *Selected Poems and Letters*, edited and translated by Margaret Rosenthal and Ann Rosalind Jones

Lucrezia Marinella, *The Nobility and Excellence of Women*, edited and translated by Anne Dunhill

Antonia Pulci, *Florentine Drama for Convent and Festival*, annotated and translated by James Wyatt Cook

Anna Maria van Schurman, *Whether a Christian Women Should Be Educated and Other Writings from Her Intellectual Circle*, edited and translated by Joyce Irwin

Arcangela Tarabotti, *Paternal Tyranny*, edited and translated by Letizia Panizza

FOREWORD

This project has gone through many phases—and years—from inception to completion, and my debts have grown with time and successive drafts. The decisive impetus for bringing the translation and introduction to publishable form was a 1994 summer research grant from the National Endowment for the Humanities and a following semester sabbatical from the State University, College at Old Westbury, for both of which I am grateful.

I have compiled many debts to individuals who have encouraged and critiqued my work. I must thank first Margaret L. King, my coeditor of this series and long-time collaborator in projects related to the Renaissance in general and to Renaissance women in particular. She first suggested that I undertake the translation of this important text and then that we oversee together the publication of a number of translations of important Renaissance texts by women from the European continent. She has subsequently served as a major critic and helped me in fashioning and refashioning both the translation and my introduction. The general introduction to the series, which will appear in each volume, was a genuinely collaborative effort, as all our joint ventures have been.

For a close reading and copious suggestions on the correction and improvement of the translation from Latin, I am deeply indebted to Jane Phillips. The suggestions of an anonymous reader also proved very helpful for additional fine tuning of the translation and its readability in English.

For an equally close reading of the introduction I am much indebted to Margaret Ferguson and Constance Jordan, whose comments, both written and oral, were instrumental in the transformation of an initial into a final draft.

Jihan Amer and Kathleen Nostrand—two among the undergraduate population for whom this and other books in the series are intended—read both the introduction and the translation and offered many suggestions in writing for the clarification of both. They have certainly done good service for me and I hope for their current and future fellow students as well.

Finally, I would like to thank my wife, Janet, who read the translation in two different recensions for its rendering of the English language, of which she is an attentive student; and for her assistance in many forms that makes my work possible.

Westbury, New York
June 23, 1995

NOTE ON THE TEXT

My translation is based on the recent critical edition by a group of French scholars: Henri Corneille Agrippa, *De nobilitate et praecellentia foeminei sexus: Edition critique d'après le texte d'Anvers 1529*, edited by R. Antonioli et al. (Geneva, 1990). I have profited from reading R. Antonioli's "Preface," which, though short on biography, is longer on the intellectual ancestry of Agrippa's declamation. My own introduction proceeded independently, however, and is quite different from that of the critical edition, though I read and reread Antonioli's preface at various points in my research and writing to check my work against his.

The critical edition prints the Latin translation first and with notes, followed by a French translation without notes. There are some errors, I assume typographical, in the Latin text. But since my translation is intended for English-speaking people unacquainted with Latin, I have not bothered to point these out. One passage included in the body of the declamation by the French editors has been relegated to a footnote in my translation, since it was added later and was not by Agrippa.

I have generally followed the notes compiled by the editors, though I have augmented them in some instances, corrected them in a few, and added notes where I thought explanations were necessary but not present in the critical edition. References to Roman and canon law have been abbreviated and presented with a view to illuminating matters discussed by Agrippa for the modern English reader. All translations from canon law are my own.

ABBREVIATIONS

ANF Ante-Nicene Fathers, ed. Alexander Roberts and James Don-
aldson, 10 vols. Grand Rapids, 1950–70.

Barnes The Complete Works of Aristotle: The Revised Oxford Translation, ed.
Jonathan Barnes, 2 vols. Princeton, 1984.

Jungmayr Henricus Cornelius Agrippa von Nettesheim, Vom Adel und Fürtreffen weibliches Geschlechts [1540], ed. Jörg Jungmayr, in Archiv für
philosophie- und theologiegeschichtliche Frauenforschung, vol. 4, Ob die
Weiber Menschen seyn, oder nicht?, ed. Elizabeth Gössmann.
Munich, 1988. German translation of Declamatio de nobilitate et
praecellentia foeminei sexus [1529].

LCL Loeb Classical Library. Cambridge, Mass. References are by
volume number of a particular author (if there is more than one
volume) followed by page number(s).

Maclean Ian Maclean, The Renaissance Notion of Woman: A Study in the Fortunes of Scholasticism and Medical Science in European Intellectual Life.
Cambridge, 1980.

Nauert Charles G. Nauert, Jr., Agrippa and the Crisis of Renaissance
Thought. Urbana, Ill., 1965.

NPNF A Select Library of Nicene and Post-Nicene Fathers, ed. Philip Schaff
et al.: series 1, Augustine and Chrysostom, 14 volumes; series
2, other post-Nicene fathers, 14 volumes. Originally published
in the 1880s, often reprinted, in the United States by William
Eerdmans.

NRSV Bible, New Revised Standard Version

PG Jacques Paul Migne, Patrologiae cursus completus . . . omnium SS. Patrum. Series Graeca, 161 vols. Paris, 1857–66. Cited when there is
no English translation.

PL Patrologiae cursus completus . . . omnium SS. patrum. Series Latina, 221
vols. plus 5 supplementary volumes. Paris, 1844–64. Cited
when there is no English translation.

Rodríguez Juan Rodríguez del Padron (or: de la Cámara), Triunfo de las Donas, in Obras Completas, ed. Cesar Hernandez Alonso. Madrid,
1982.

Scott The Civil Law, trans. S. P. Scott, 17 vols. Cincinnati, 1932. 1:
The Twelve Tables; 2–11: Digest; 12–15: Code; 16–17:
Novels.

DECLAMATION ON THE
NOBILITY AND PREEMINENCE
OF THE FEMALE SEX

AGRIPPA AND
THE FEMINIST TRADITION

THE OTHER VOICE IN
AGRIPPA'S DECLAMATION ON WOMEN

In 1509 Henricus Cornelius Agrippa delivered at the University of Dôle a Latin declamation on the nobility and preeminence of women. Although in some respects he had predecessors, his declamation was, in more important respects, original. Not content with simply cataloguing renowned women of the past—as had been done by his most famous classical predecessor, Plutarch, and his most famous Renaissance predecessor, Boccaccio[1] —Agrippa argued that women were the equals of men in all things that really counted, including public spheres of activity from which they had long been excluded. He raised the question of why women were excluded and provided answers based not on sex but on social conditioning, education, and the prejudices of their more powerful oppressors. Ironically, Agrippa did not believe that his declamation was among the more important of his works. In this respect he resembles Erasmus of Rotterdam (1467–1536), whose *Moriae Encomium* (*Praise of Folly*, written 1509, published 1511) is today the most widely read of his many books.

Nonetheless, when his declamation was published in 1529—among the first of his writings to be printed—it was almost immediately translated into French, English, Italian, and German. His influence throughout the sixteenth century was enormous and continued into the following century, and his text was plagiarized all over Europe. It is fair to say that the influence of his work *On Occult Philosophy* or his treatise *On the Uncertainty and Vanity of the Sciences*

---

1. Plutarch (46–120 CE) is much cited by Renaissance authors, including Agrippa, both from his lives of famous men and from his moral essays. With regard to women his most-cited text is *Bravery of Women* (LCL, *Moralia*, 3:473–581). Boccaccio (1313–75) devoted several works to women, the most famous his *De claris mulieribus* (*Concerning Famous Women*, 1355–59), containing biographies of famous women, primarily from pagan antiquity. This text was important for subsequent writers for several centuries, Agrippa among them.

and Arts, both of which remained influential over an extended period of time, can be matched by that of the short declamation translated here. And yet its influence has not been recognized, perhaps because its subject was not considered important until the present generation. Charles Nauert's 1965 biography fails to mention it at all in discussing Agrippa's influence.

Wherein lay its power? Evidently in the confluence of two factors: Agrippa's own personality and his use of paradox to overturn the misogynistic interpretations of the female body in Greek medicine, the Bible, Roman and canon law, theology and moral philosophy, and politics. His citations of famous women—drawn from classical Greek and Roman as well as Jewish and Christian antiquity—were employed to reinforce his arguments rather than merely catalogue famous (and in some respects anomalous) women.

AGRIPPA'S LIFE AND WORKS

Cornelius Agrippa's life may conveniently be divided into four periods: his education and early fame, 1486–1510; his sojourn in Italy, 1511–18; his failed expectations and depression, 1518–28; and the publication of his works, 1529–35.[2] The first period, which included his declamation on women, was dominated by his study of occult philosophy and ended with the completion of *De occulta philosophia* (*On Occult Philosophy,* 1510), which formed the cornerstone of his fame in his own day and later. He was born in Cologne on September 14, 1486, and matriculated at its university on July 22, 1499, not yet quite 13. He received his licentiate in arts on March 14, 1502, the only recorded degree he ever earned.[3] The years between 1502 and 1507 (when his correspondence begins) have left no record. After he left Cologne he led a wandering life during which "he resided in no country more than seven years, and in no city as many as four."[4] By 1507 he was in Paris. But then between 1507 and 1509 he was involved in some intrigue in Spain, apparently in the employ of the Emperor Maximilian.

In 1509 Agrippa was back in France, where he delivered the lecture

2. On Agrippa's life, in addition to Nauert, chaps. 1–5 (pp. 8–115), see Thomas P. Deutscher, "Henricus Cornelius Agrippa," in Peter G. Bietenholz and Thomas P. Deutscher, eds., *Contemporaries of Erasmus: A Biographical Register of the Renaissance and Reformation,* 3 vols. (Toronto, 1985–87), 1:17–19; and R. Schmitz, in *Dictionary of Scientific Biography,* ed. C. C. Gillispie, et al. (New York, 1970–80), 1:79–81.

3. Nauert nonetheless surmises that he was telling the truth when he claimed to have doctorates in both laws (civil and canon). See 10–11.

4. Ibid., 6.

translated here, which served as introduction to a course of lectures on Johann Reuchlin's *De verbo mirifico* (*On the Miraculous Word*).[5] Although only 23, Agrippa was already well known by this time for his interest in the *prisca theologia* or ancient theology, which stretched from Moses through the wise men of Egypt (Hermes Trismegistus), Persia (Zoroaster), Greece (Orpheus and Pythagoras down to Plato and the Platonists). In the late fifteenth century these texts were translated into Latin by the Florentine philosopher Marsilio Ficino (1433–99) and interpreted in commentaries by Ficino and his colleague Giovanni Pico della Mirandola (1462–93). These ancient writers were believed to possess a wisdom that, if revealed, would be the key to great power. Charles Nauert, Agrippa's major modern biographer, describes Agrippa's synoptic vision of philosophy:

> The world view of Agrippa is that of Hellenistic and medieval times. All parts of the universe are closely connected, for the superior rules its immediate inferior and is ruled by its own superior; at the top of this hierarchy, the Archetype, God, reigns supreme, transmitting His power down through the entire system. The human soul may ascend through this hierarchy and so attain the power of the superior ranks, even the power of God. This doctrine of mystical ascent through a hierarchy of being is one basis for magic. The other basis is the belief that all being is so closely linked that whatever affects one part affects all the others. The world may thus be compared to a great living animal, all of which is affected when any member is affected. Or, to use a simile which Agrippa himself employs, the sympathy among its parts is like that between two harps tuned to the same pitch. If one harp is struck, the strings of the other will also vibrate.[6]

Agrippa's lectures were well attended. He was aiming at a regular faculty position at Dôle and might have succeeded in obtaining one but for a charge by Jean Catilinet, the provincial superior of the Franciscans in Burgundy, that Agrippa was "a Judaizing heretic, who has introduced into Christian schools the criminal, condemned, and prohibited art of Kabbala, who, despising the holy fathers and Catholic doctors, prefer the rabbis of the Jews, and bend sacred letters to heretical arts and the Talmud of the Jews."[7] Agrippa re-

5. On Reuchlin, in addition to what follows, see the translation, n. 4.

6. Nauert, 265.

7. The quotation is from Agrippa's defense against Catilinet, *Expostulatio contra Catilinetum*, in *Opera*, 2:509; cited by Nauert, 28.

sponded in characteristic fashion that he was not a heretic, adding that he also did not condemn rabbinical learning.

Catilinet's attack reflected a negative attitude toward Jewish literature that had been growing in the theological faculty at Dôle.[8] It was growing elsewhere as well. One year after Agrippa's lectures the Pfefferkorn–Reuchlin controversy broke out. Johann Pfefferkorn (1469–1521), a Christian converted from Judaism, demanded of the emperor that all Jewish books be confiscated and destroyed. Emperor Maximilian called for biblical scholars to advise him, and Johann Reuchlin was the only scholar who responded by defending Jewish books, arguing that only two were attacks on Christianity and that the rabbis had suppressed these; all the others were harmless. Pfefferkorn then attacked Reuchlin, who responded in kind. The Dominicans and the theologians of Cologne supported Pfefferkorn, while most of the humanists supported Reuchlin. After 1517 the quarrel was caught up in the controversies surrounding Luther and the Reformation. Pope Leo X finally ruled against Reuchlin in 1520, though Reuchlin remained unharmed except for the great expenses incurred in defending himself.[9]

In 1510 Agrippa visited the Abbot Trithemius (1462–1516), one of the most famous occult philosophers in Agrippa's native Germany, who encouraged him to continue his pursuit of the ancient wisdom; later in the same year he completed the initial version of *On Occult Philosophy*, which he dedicated to Trithemius. That work circulated in manuscript among intellectuals for many years until the eventual publication in 1533 of a greatly augmented edition. Also in 1510 he visited John Colet (1467–1519), one of England's most famous humanists and churchmen, with whom he studied the Pauline epistles. It was while in London that he wrote his response to the attack of Catilinet.

The second period of Agrippa's life was the years he spent in Italy, 1511–18. He seems initially to have served a military function for the Emperor Maximilian, but his principal interest remained the ancient theology. In 1515 he lectured at Pavia on the hermetic *Pimander*. In the treatises composed in Italy—*Oratio in praelectione convivii Platonis* (*Oration on the Reading of Plato's Symposium*, ca. 1515), *De triplici ratione cognoscendi Deum* (*On the Three Ways of Knowing God*, ca. 1516), and *Dialogus de homine* (*Dialogue on Man*, 1516)—the theme is faith in the Hermetic writings, now restored through the work of Ficino.

8. Nauert, 28–29.

9. See IG [sic], "Johann Pfefferkorn," *Contemporaries of Erasmus*, 3:76–77, and sources cited; and Heinz Scheible, "Johann Reuchlin," ibid., 3:145–50, and sources cited.

While in Italy Agrippa also contracted the first of his three marriages, to an Italian woman from Pavia; a son was born to the couple in 1517.[10]

The third period of Agrippa's life was what we might call a period of middle-age crisis. Though it may have had little to do with age and much more to do with Agrippa's personality and to circumstance, it was filled with conflicts, disappointments, and even depression. Things began auspiciously enough. He returned from Italy to assume the position of orator and lawyer in the free imperial city of Metz. Here his penchant for going against received ideas began to cause him difficulty. Before February 1519 he wrote *De originali peccato* (*On Original Sin*), in which he maintained—against orthodox opinion—that the original sin had been an act of sexual intercourse between Adam and Eve.[11] Even more significant were several disputes in which he became involved that were inevitably interpreted in relation to the newly emergent Lutheran Reformation. Agrippa read some of Luther's writings, and although he never sided with the Reformation, some of the friends he later left behind in Metz did.[12] More immediately significant to him, he defended a woman accused of witchcraft (proving, among other things, that her accusers had contrived to rob her of her property).[13] He also achieved some notoriety—culminating in his being denounced from the pulpit as a heretic—for defending the view of the French humanist Jacques Lefèvre d'Étaples (1455–1536) that St. Anne, the mother of Mary, was not (as medi-

10. In 1519 he praised her as "a noble maiden, a well behaved and beautiful young woman, [who] lives so to my taste that up to now not a harsh word has passed between us, and, I trust, never will" (quoted in Nauert, 40).

11. For an interesting discussion of it, see James G. Turner, *One Flesh: Paradisal Marriage and Sexual Relations in the Age of Milton* (New York, 1987), 157–60; see also Nauert, 58 and 58 n. 5.

12. Nauert, 65–67.

13. In *Of the Vanitie and Uncertaintie of Artes and Sciences*, ed. Catherine M. Dunn (Northridge, Calif., 1974), chap. 96, Agrippa gives an account of this case. The Inquisitor argued his case first on the grounds of law, then of reason. Agrippa countered with the groundlessness of the accusations in either form. As to the first, the argument that the woman's mother had been burned as a witch, Agrippa pointed out that in law this was no ground to accuse another person. As to the second, when the Inquisitor cited the *Malleus Maleficarum* as the source for his accusations, Agrippa accused him in turn of simply using that text as a means of taking advantage of a poor country woman and countered with the assertion that Christ had redeemed us all from sin. Although the Inquisitor became angry, the end result was that the case was dismissed and the accusers were forced to pay a large sum of money to the charter of the church of Metz, whose subjects they were (*Of the Vanitie and Uncertaintie of Artes and Sciences*, 351–52).

Nauert (59) points out that Agrippa does not attack the reality of witchcraft itself, but he rightly adds that such a procedure would hardly have been effective. Brian Copenhaver makes the same point (*Symphorien Champier and the Reception of the Occultist Tradition in Renaissance France* [The Hague, 1978], 157).

eval tradition had embellished the matter) also the mother of two other daughters by two later marriages, all three daughters named Mary. The ensuing controversy eventually made Agrippa's stay in Metz uncomfortable, and he left in 1520, though he was in the city in the spring of 1521 when his wife died.

Later that year he began a two-year stay in Geneva, where he married a second time (November 1521). His French wife bore him four sons and a daughter before she died in 1529. His daughter and one son died young. At least three sons (Aymon, Henri, and Jean) outlived him, settling in France. About his second wife he wrote after her death: "There was never anger between us upon which the sun set." Earlier he had called her noble and beautiful and said that he could not decide whether she or his first wife was more loving and obedient,[14] a comment that betrays conventional attitudes toward women.

He believed he had found the more lucrative employment he had been seeking when he was invited in 1524 to the French court, where he took up residence in Lyon as personal physician to Louise of Savoy, the queen mother.[15] He remained there for almost four years (his longest residence in any one place since childhood). His first two years were pleasant enough, but then he managed to offend his patroness by refusing her request that he cast a horoscope for the king. The moment was a tense one in France: Francis had lost the battle of Pavia and was taken prisoner by the Spanish in 1525. Louise ran the country in his absence during 1525–26, effectively protecting his interests. He had only recently been restored to his throne when the queen mother made her request. Not only did Agrippa refuse to cast the horoscope, suggesting that the queen mother put her talents to better use than to engage in "astrological superstition," but he went on indiscreetly to suggest (in a letter shown to the queen mother) that if he had cast a horoscope it would have been unfavorable to the king and favorable to his archrival, the duke of Bour-

---

14. Nauert, 71.

15. Louise (1476–1531) was the wife of Charles of Valois, who died in 1496, leaving her with two children: Margaret (b. 1492) and Francis (b. 1494). Francis become king in 1515. From then until her death Louise played an important role in governing the country. When Francis left to fight in 1515 and again in 1525, he appointed his mother regent. During this period she rejected efforts to abrogate the Concordat of Bologna (1516) giving the king power to appoint bishops in France. She was a *politique*, showing little of the interest in religious reform exhibited by her daughter Margaret (see n. 17). She negotiated the Peace of Cambrai with Margaret of Austria (to whom Agrippa dedicated his declamation on women) in 1529, bringing to a close the war between Francis and Charles V. The duke of Bourbon rebelled in 1523 and was still Francis's principal internal enemy in 1526 when Louise asked Agrippa to cast the king's horoscope. See Gordon Griffiths, "Louise of Savoy," *Contemporaries of Erasmus*, 3:201–2, and sources cited.

bon. Agrippa's indiscretion included the prediction that the king would die within six months.[16] It is therefore not surprising that he was cut off from the court and that his last year or so in France was lived in great poverty and increasing bitterness.

His unhappiness did not prevent him from attempting to regain favor at court, and to that end he dedicated to Margaret of Angoulême (1492–1549), sister of Francis I, queen of Navarre, and author of the *Heptameron*,[17] his *De sacramento matrimonii declamatio* (*Declamation on the Sacrament of Marriage*, 1526), in which he argued that everyone (except those who are naturally cold and the professionally religious) should marry to avoid fornication. He attributed the latter especially to men and not, as did the mainstream tradition, primarily to women. He maintained that marriage has not only procreation but companionship as its purpose, that people should therefore marry for love, and that children should not be forced by their parents to marry someone against their will. He contended here as in his earlier declamation on the nobility of women that evil wives happen only to evil husbands. The treatise was criticized for its heterodoxy and did not achieve its aim, even though Agrippa tried to defend it and even translate it into the vernacular.

Two of his most important works were composed in the aftermath of his despair: *Dehortatio gentilis theologiae* (*Against Pagan Theology*, June 1526), in which he argued for the primacy of faith over reason; and *De incertitudine et vanitate scientiarum declamatio invectiva* (*On the Uncertainty and Vanity of the Sciences and Arts*, late summer, 1526), the most widely circulated and best known of his works. In it he renounced all human arts and sciences, even those he had treated in *On Occult Philosophy*, stressing the superiority of the Christian gospel over all human learning.

Virtually all that Agrippa was to write had now been written. During the last phase of his life—among his happiest years—his major accomplishment was overseeing the publication of his works. He began this task in 1529 when he was finally permitted to leave France and make his way to Antwerp. His initial happiness there was marred by the death of his wife from the plague in August 1529.

Agrippa's declamation on women, written and delivered in 1509, was

16. See Nauert, 94.

17. Margaret was active in Francis's court as a patron of men of letters from 1515 until the 1530s. Until the affair of the placards in 1534 she was involved with religious reformers as well but thereafter retired to her estates and surrounded herself with men of letters. It was during this last period of her life that she composed the *Heptameron* (published 1559). See Henry Heller, "Margaret of Angoulême," *Contemporaries of Erasmus*, 2:386–88 and sources cited

among the first of his works to be published. It led to his appointment, on December 27, 1529, as imperial archivist and historiographer at the court of Margaret of Austria.[18] Margaret did not, however, continue to favor him. In 1530 the first of many editions of *Vanity* was published. Infuriated by its attack on monks, Margaret, without Agrippa's knowledge, sent the book to the theological faculty of Louvain for examination on September 1, 1530. Had she not died on December 1, 1530, Agrippa might well have been prosecuted for impiety, though attacks on monks challenged no church doctrine and hence were not heretical.[19]

In June 1532 Agrippa moved to Cologne, where he published a much expanded edition of *On Occult Philosophy* in June 1533 (book 1 had been published in 1531). His last letters date from this period. Later accounts of his life suggest that he married a third time but shortly thereafter divorced his wife and moved to France, first to Lyon and then to Grenoble, where he died in obscurity and was buried in 1535. A complete edition of his works was published in Lyon around 1600 (reprinted 1970).

Agrippa seems to be a classic case of the divided consciousness. On the one hand he believed in the power of the occult to gain control over the universe; on the other he was skeptical of knowing anything at all. How do we reconcile—or do we—these two sides of his personality?

The presence of the apparently contradictory elements of magic and skepticism in the thought of the same man was disturbing to many in Agrippa's own time. The doubts expressed in *Vanity* helped to mold the legend of Faust—Christopher Marlowe made Agrippa his model in his drama *The Tragical History of Doctor Faustus* (1595).[20] More than two centuries later Goethe, creator of yet another Faust, was profoundly shaken by reading *Vanity*.[21] In an apology written to protect the book from attacks of the Louvain theologians, Agrippa said that he "was only declaiming," that much of what he had said had been in jest.[22] He said the same about his lecture on

---

18. "His official writings consist of a history of the coronation of Charles V as king of the Lombards and emperor of the Romans at Bologna in February, 1530, a work which merely lists the order of processions; a funeral oration composed later in 1530 for his patron, Margaret of Austria; and a speech of welcome to the Emperor written for the latter's nephew, Prince John of Denmark" (Nauert, 105).

19. Ibid., 107, 177–78.

20. See Christopher Marlowe, *The Complete Plays*, ed. J. B. Steane (New York, 1969).

21. Nauert, 195. See Goethe, *Faust*, trans. Walter Kaufmann (Garden City, N.Y., 1961), part 1 and sections from part 2.

22. Nauert, 196.

women.[23] Many critics have been led to the conclusion that Agrippa did not intend either the lecture on women or *Vanity* to be taken seriously, that is, that he did not believe what he said.

Agrippa's major modern biographer argues that the contradiction in Agrippa's thought is only apparent,[24] that "distrust in the powers of the human mind to attain truth was the basic presupposition of occultism rather than the product of disillusionment with it."[25] Even Agrippa's earliest interest in occult philosophy was based on a fundamental doubt concerning the powers of the human mind and an attempt to escape it through the authority of antiquity, specifically, the mystical antiquity of Neoplatonism, a philosophy dedicated not only to an understanding of the cosmos but also to the ascent of the individual soul to God. Agrippa long maintained the hope that on the next page he read his doubts might be assuaged. Not only did this not happen, but he was exposed to more eroding influences. One was biblical fideism, the view that faith in the Bible as the word of God did not require rational justification. Another was ancient skepticism, in its more dogmatic form the view that knowledge was impossible, and in its undogmatic form the view that judgment had to be suspended on the question of whether knowledge could be attained about anything. These influences were paramount in *Vanity*. His final refuge was a mystical experience, but since he confessed that he had never had such an experience, he was left in limbo. Nauert concludes that "Agrippa's mind drifted uncertainly between intellectual despair on the one hand and a sort of omnivorous, generalized credulity on the other."[26]

Agrippa's lecture on women is a confirmation of Nauert's analysis: it was delivered at about the time that he wrote *On Occult Philosophy* (1510), which holds out the possibility of total knowledge, but it expresses a skepticism

23. See the dedicatory letter to the councillor Maximilian of Transylvania, which precedes his declamation.

24. "Almost all the standard histories of philosophy mention the presence of skeptical elements in his thought, although they generally class him among Neoplatonic occultists or theosophists, and although they agree that his skepticism is only fragmentary and not of much significance. One of the few writers who has taken the skeptical side of his thought seriously . . . explains this apparent contradiction by assuming a fundamental change of attitude. . . . Actually, however, there was no major change" (Nauert, 293–94).

25. Ibid., 201; also 237: "Only long experience could teach man what were the real forces working in the universe, and how they could be controlled. Hence, there was a natural association between a skeptical attitude toward rational knowledge and a lively interest in the occult arts."

This seems to be the conclusion reached as well by Michael H. Keefer, "Agrippa's Dilemma: Hermetic 'Rebirth' and the Ambivalences of *De vanitate* and *De occulta philosophia*," *Renaissance Quarterly* 41 (1988), 614–53.

26. Nauert, 262.

toward received wisdom characteristic of *Vanity* (1526). In the opening chapter of the latter, for example, he asserts that "all sciences are nothing but decisions and opinions of men" and adds later "that anything can be disproved just as easily as it can be proved, that there is no argument so strong that a stronger cannot be presented to overturn it."[27] When Agrippa treats legal and political institutions he emphasizes that laws are arbitrary, based on the wills of lawmakers; in saying this he makes no distinction between pagan and Mosaic law. And not only the Christian Old Testament but the apostles of the New can be judged to have fallen away from the truth.[28] Indeed, "every man is a liar; but only Christ, man and God, never was and never will be found untruthful."[29] If the Bible shares the limitations of every other book (an astounding attitude at the time), how much more is this true for theologians, philosophers, medical practitioners, and lawyers? "If men be the inventors of Sciences, is not every man a liar, neither is there one that does good?"[30]

Although the ultimate test of truth is Jesus Christ, the problem is how, if traditional authorities of church and Bible as foundations of truth are questioned, Jesus Christ is accessible. The only other avenue to truth Agrippa accepts is experience gained through the senses. He acknowledges that what can be known must agree with the senses and that by the senses we are led to such things as can be known. But the senses can be deceived and cannot prove anything with certainty; nor can they give us the causes of things, so that ultimate truth is not accessible to the senses—and so not accessible at all.[31] We can know some truth but not the Truth.

Both his skepticism with regard to past authorities and his empiricism are evident in Agrippa's declamation on women. His arguments all follow from several major premises: that the oppression of women supported by medical practitioners, philosophers, the Bible, theologians, and lawyers has been based on custom; that all customs are arbitrary, so that there is no theoretical justification for the status quo; and that, using the texts on which op-

---

27. The first statement is quoted in Nauert; the second, based on an assertion in *Vanity*, chap. 100, is Nauert's, both 297. In *Vanity*, chap. 54, Agrippa repeats these ideas. Moral philosophy, he says, "depends not so much on the reasons of philosophers as on varying usage, custom, observation, and frequent use of daily living, and is changeable according to the opinion of times, places, and men . . ." (quoted, ibid., 308).

28. "The Doctors of the New Testament are the Apostles, and Evangelists, and although all these were replenished with the Holy Ghost, notwithstanding all did in some place swerve from the truth, and . . . they were liars . . ." (*Vanitie*, chap. 99, 367).

29. *Vanity*, chap. 99 (quoted in Nauert, 305).

30. *Vanitie*, chap. 1, 13.

31. See *Vanitie*, chap. 7, 49.

pressive interpretations have been based, one may just as well arrive at opposite conclusions.

Agrippa's declamation bears out these conclusions. He sets out to demolish all received wisdom regarding women from every authoritative source and proves the opposite. The opposite of the inferior status of women is not their equality with men but their superiority, and so that becomes his thesis. Agrippa succeeded in getting everyone's attention, as well as in leading many to follow in his footsteps and plagiarize his work. The question of the seriousness of his intent pales in the face of the literature it inspired and the importance of that literature in molding new attitudes that would eventually bear fruit.

CONTENT AND ANALYSIS OF THE DECLAMATION

The translation is divided into ten sections for the convenience of the English reader; there are no divisions in Agrippa's Latin text. The content of the declamation can be briefly summarized. Agrippa opens by stating his agreement with the philosophical and theological tradition that men and women have the same soul (belong to the same species). But he draws conclusions very different from those of his predecessors. In the order of creation women are superior, and their superiority involves the following, discussed in succession: the name, being the last earthly creature created (and so the first in conception, the fulfillment or perfection of the whole), being created in Paradise (rather than outside it as Adam was), being created from a superior material (part of Adam rather than dirt). The creation accounts of both Genesis 1 and 2 are turned to the advantage of women. The superior beauty of woman is demonstrated by her greater closeness to God than men can claim. Her physical beauty—described in painstaking detail—is indicative also of spiritual beauty. God has made nothing in the world more beautiful, which is why all love women. This claim is illustrated from both classical and biblical sources. The many virtues of women also point to their superiority; these are modesty, purity, primary role in procreation, piety and compassion, greater capacity for sex, positive qualities of pregnancy and menstruation, ability to conceive without a male, superior eloquence. Not only does Scripture confirm these virtues, but Scripture also proves, by contrast, that original sin came through Adam, not Eve. Christ took the form of a male because it was men who needed redeeming. But Christ chose to be born of a woman without a man; and he appeared first to women after his resurrection. Scripture further proves the superiority of women by looking more favorably on the evil actions of women than on the good actions of men (a discussion that reverses Ecclus. 42:14, which states that the evil actions of men are better than the good actions of women). Many examples from Scripture (from which the opposite point of view was derived) confirm the assertion. Capping this argument with the declaration that the noblest of all creatures was a woman (the Virgin Mary), the most wicked a man (Judas), Agrippa is led naturally into proving, also from Scripture and by many examples, the greater wickedness of men. By contrast, that women are more generous and chaste, more faithful in conjugal love, more modest and pious, is proved by many examples. Counterexamples that would disprove the contention are also cited, but the women in these instances are exonerated on the ground that when they are evil the fault is that of men who made them so. Women first vowed their virginity to God, have been more inspired prophets than men, and have suffered martyrdom courageously. The constancy of some has led to the naming of books of the Bible after them. Women have been responsible for the conversion of many peoples to Christianity. Their activity in the world, in fact, parallels in every kind of accomplishment that of men. Women have been priestesses, prophets, magicians, and philosophers; they have written poetry and legal briefs and are masters of oratory; they have excelled in dialectics and medicine; they have demonstrated great wisdom and ruled kingdoms; they have been the founders of empires with their inventions of letters and the arts; they have saved nations by their courage. Women played an important role in the founding of Rome and were always honored there—this latter illustrated by many examples. There have been cultures in which the roles now played by men and women in our culture have been reversed. It is social custom, based on the tyranny of men, that has prevented and prevents women from taking on public offices and responsibilities.

As this summary of Agrippa's declamation suggests, his oration moves by a series of contrasts in which qualities and actions of men and women are compared to one another. A striking feature of the comparisons is the extent to which Agrippa appeals to Scripture to "prove" his case for the superiority of women. His use of Scripture is evident from the very beginning, where he cites Genesis 1:27 (a text avoided by misogynists) in saying that men and women are equal in soul. While this text agrees with Aristotle and Aquinas that men and women belong to the same species, in implying equality it departs from them in every other respect. In particular it leads Agrippa to interpret the creation story in Genesis 2—much cited by misogynists—in light of Genesis 1. Ideas expressed here about the place and matter of creation were medieval commonplaces. The following, for example, appears in a thirteenth-century manuscript:

Woman is to be preferred to man, clearly for the following reasons: *Matter*: Because Adam was created from the muddy earth, Eve from the side of Adam. *Place*: Because Adam was created outside paradise, Eve within paradise. *In Conception*: Because woman conceived God, man being unable to do so. *Appearance*: Because Christ first appeared to a woman after the resurrection, namely, to Mary Magdalene. *Exaltation*: Because a woman is exalted above the choir of angels, namely, the blessed Virgin Mary.[32]

Such commonplaces were doubtless familiar to Agrippa's audience. But Agrippa builds on these commonplaces much more substantial claims. For one thing, the fact that Adam was a product of nature while Eve was created directly by God, leads him to the conclusion that woman is more capable than man of receiving the divine light. Agrippa's theoretical assertions here, as throughout his declamation, are followed by empirical examples which add weight to his argument, in this case of the love of the gods and goddesses for mortals in classical antiquity and of men for women as recounted in the Hebrew Bible.

The arguments for the superiority of female virtue, drawn from various sources, are only apparently fantastic. Their underlying theme is that women are more modest than men: their long hair conceals shameful body parts, women do not need to touch these body parts when they urinate, these parts do not protrude in women as they do in men, women are loath to expose their body parts to a male physician and have been known to choose death rather than to do so, women float face down in water when drowned, their heads (the supreme part of the human body) are never bald, they secrete menses from the lower parts of their bodies while male secretions are from the face, they are always clean after one washing (while men continue to dirty the water no matter how many times they wash and change the water), and when they fall they fall on their backs and not on their faces.

These physiological "facts" lead Agrippa naturally into matters that concerned medical experts. He sides with Galen against Aristotle on the ques-

---

32. Paul Meyer, "Mélanges de poésie française," *Romania* 6 (1877), 501. The Latin reads: Mulier prefertur viro, scilicet: *Materia*: Quia Adam factus de limo terre, Eva de costa Ade. *Loco*: Quia Adam factus extra paradisum, Eva in paradiso. *In conceptione*: Quia mulier concepit Deum, quod homo non potuit. *Apparicione*: Quia Christus primo apparvit mulieri post resurrectionem, scilicet Magdalene. *Exaltacione*: Quia mulier exaltata est super choros angelorum, scilicet beata Maria.

Christine de Pizan also cites a version of it: "Now, to turn to the question of the creation of the body, woman was made by the Supreme Craftsman. In what place was she created? In the Terrestrial Paradise. From what substance? Was it vile matter? No, it was the noblest substance which had ever been created: it was from the body of man from which God made woman" (*Book of the City of Ladies*, 23–24).

tion of whether females produce semen, but he shows himself more radical than most Galenists of his time in arguing not only that women contribute semen in procreation but that their semen is more efficacious than that of the male. Woman's heat is also efficacious, as it was for David in his old age, an argument aimed at Aristotle's notion that cold and moist humors predominate in women.[33]

Agrippa suggests that women are more virile (in the sense of stronger) than men in adding that a woman is ready for procreation at an earlier age than a male is and that she is inclined to sexual activity even after she becomes pregnant and not long after she has delivered a child. He turns the Platonic conception of the womb as an autonomous creature—intended to prove how fragile women were—into an argument for the power of women: when pregnant she can eat raw fish, even dirt or poison, without suffering harmful consequences. He adds as well the efficacy of menstrual blood—it has power to cure many illnesses, both physical and psychological— whereas most of the tradition of doctors and philosophers had emphasized its dangerous tendencies and harmful consequences.[34] The most astonishing testimony of female power is the ability of a woman to reproduce without the assistance of a man. Though he discredits accounts from the Muslim tradition, he credits the Christian account of the virgin birth, to which, in fact, he returns several times. So much for the inferiority of women based on physical attributes.

Agrippa challenges the psychology as well as the physiology of Aristotle. He cites the amazing properties of women's milk as evidence of their greater piety; Aristotle had said that women are more compassionate and merciful, though he had not regarded these as necessarily positive attributes, as Agrippa does. Further, Agrippa argues that children are more like their mothers than their fathers in character: if their mothers are wise, so are their children, and vice versa, though wise fathers often beget stupid children; naturally, then, we love our mothers more than we love our fathers, because there is more of our mothers than of our fathers in us. All of these contentions are direct contradictions of Aristotle's psychology. But the capstone of his

---

33. See the translation, n. 50.

34. "Nearly all the encyclopedists repeated the litany, taken by Isidore of Seville from Pliny and transmitted to the Middle Ages, about the nefarious effects of menstrual blood. That foul substance was blamed for preventing seeds from germinating, for turning grape mash bitter, for killing herbs, for causing trees to shed their fruit, for rusting iron and blackening brass, for giving dogs rabies. It could even dissolve pitch too hard to be scraped away with iron" (Claude Thomasset, "The Nature of Woman," *A History of Women in the West*, vol. 1, ed. Pauline Schmitt Pantel [Cambridge, Mass., 1992], 65).

attack on Greek female psychology is his reply to Aristotle's well-known assertion that men are more courageous, wise, and noble than women; he counters with the Pauline passage, of which Erasmus made such brilliant use in *Praise of Folly*, that God chose the foolish things of this world to confound the wise, the weak to confound the strong, the despised to reduce to nothing things that are.

The more positive aspects of female psychology lead to a reassessment as well of her mental capacities, for example her superior eloquence. Reversing one of the most pervasively derisive of misogynistic commonplaces, Agrippa argues that women are more fluent, eloquent, and effusive in speech than men. The proof is that we learn to speak from our mothers or nurses and that one hardly ever finds a mute woman. The fact that women are superior to men in precisely that trait in which humans are superior to all other animals is testimony to her superiority over all other creatures. Indeed, women have been the inventors of all the liberal arts. Isis and Nicostrata have given us the alphabet and writing, Minerva (Athena) numbers, as well as wool- and ironmaking. The very continents have been named for women. Women have made significant contributions to religion as priestesses and prophets, to magic and philosophy, to oratory and poetry. The Virgin Mary was the first to vow her virginity to God; Scripture attests to women prophets and celebrates the constancy of women such as Judith, Ruth, Esther, and the mother (in 2 and 4 Macc.) who watched her seven sons martyred for their fidelity to the Jewish law and then followed them into martyrdom. More recent history attests the important role of women in the conversion of Europe to Christianity.

Women have thus been the source of a blessing to men. Scripture asserts that God blessed man because of woman (Abraham because of Sarah, Jacob because of Rebecca). Agrippa reverses the misogynistic use of 1 Corinthians 11:7, where Paul says that man is the glory of God while woman is the glory of man. Agrippa cites only the assertion that woman is the glory of man and then adds that glory is by definition a point of completion and perfection.

But while woman has given us a blessing, man has given us the law, the curse, and the wrath of God. Original sin came into the world through Adam, to whom alone the fruit of the tree had been prohibited, and Adam's (not Eve's) sin brought death to us all—here he cites Romans 5:12 and 1 Corinthians 15:42–49 to advantage. Moreover, the man sinned in knowledge, the woman only in ignorance, and hence Adam's sin was greater than Eve's. Christ was born a man in order to expiate the sin of the first man—atonement had to come through the sex that had sinned. Agrippa also explains the conferral of the priesthood on men alone in the same way: priests represent Christ who represents Adam. Moreover, he adds, men abandoned Christ after his death, but no women did, and men have been responsible for all the heresies. Imagine the evil things women would have been able to write about men if they had had the power to write histories!

As he concludes his declamation, Agrippa makes a valiant effort to show that the strictures that prevent women from performing in the world in his day were not always in effect. In Roman antiquity women achieved greatness in areas in which they are not now allowed to act. He cites a number of pagan priestesses as well as prophetesses from the Bible, practitioners of magic, philosophers and disciples of famous male philosophers, orators, poets, and grammarians, women who ruled kingdoms with unsurpassed wisdom, and women who exhibited great courage in saving their lands from enemy attacks. He concludes his catalogue with Joan of Arc (1412–31) as a woman near his own time who exhibited qualities of wisdom and courage characteristic of classical women, proving that these qualities in women did not perish with the women of antiquity. Not only did women achieve greatness in antiquity, but they were recognized and rewarded, as Roman law and ancient historians attest. In his own day, Agrippa says, women are not active participants in public life, not because they are incapable but because of the tyranny of men, unjust laws, custom, and lack of education. Idleness is today enforced for women. They are kept in the home and out of the public (including the ecclesiastical) arena—all against divine right and natural law.

At every possible point—against doctors, philosophers, and theologians —Agrippa reverses traditions of interpretation, proving, as he said in *Vanity*, that one can prove the opposite of anything with equal plausibility. He did not say—though he implied—that all this should be changed. Actually to have advocated change would have been as futile as defending the accused witch of Metz by challenging belief in witchcraft; it probably did not even occur to him to do so.

AGRIPPA'S KNOWLEDGE OF THE FEMINIST TRADITION

What sources did Agrippa actually use? We know that he was a very learned man, widely read and adept at languages, claiming degrees in law, medicine, and theology. That he was also highly respected for his learning is clear from the fact that he delivered public lectures at the University of Dôle when he was only twenty-three. As notes to the translation make clear, he was intimately familiar with the major philosophical and literary texts of antiquity related to the debate about women; he ranges widely over many fields of learning in culling arguments and examples, especially the latter. Moreover, he was widely traveled, living at various times in Spain, France, and Italy, where the major contemporary developments in the *querelle des femmes* were taking place.

He was certainly familiar with Boccaccio's *Concerning Famous Women*, from which some of his examples are drawn. Whether he was also familiar with Boccaccio's *Corbaccio*, a notoriously misogynist text, is not clear. Both these texts stand at the beginning of the traditions that inaugurate "the other voice." *Concerning Famous Women* was familiar to all writers on the subject after Boccaccio, and the *Corbaccio* inspired much of the Spanish literature that takes the form of the defense of women's honor.

Was he familiar as well with Christine de Pizan, either the debate over *Le Roman de la rose* (*The Romance of the Rose*) in which she took part or her *Le Livre de la Cité des dames* (*The Book of the City of Ladies*)? Neither existed in printed form, though the latter at least was well circulated in manuscript among the learned in France. There is no direct evidence that he knew of her work, though her views were "in the air" in France where Agrippa delivered his lecture. He might well have been aware of this fact in choosing the subject of a declamation dedicated to a ruling female monarch.

From the courtly love tradition it is possible to document Agrippa's familiarity with Rodríguez del Padron's *Triunfo de las donas* (*Triumph of Women*). Rodríguez was born around the turn of the fifteenth century into the minor Galician nobility. As a young man he served at the court of Juan II (1406–54) and became a page of the future Cardinal Juan de Cervantes. Sometime during his stay at court he fell in love with a woman of higher station, an intriguingly mysterious affair since he never divulged her identity. The indiscretion of a trusted friend cost him his lady's affection and led to his banishment from court. In 1430 we find him "in exile" traveling with Cardinal Cervantes. He was in the cardinal's company in 1431 when the latter attended the church council at Basel. There he may well have met Enea Silvio Piccolomini, the future Pope Pius II (1458–64), whose own *Historia de duobus amantibus* (*The Story of Two Lovers*) may have influenced Rodríguez's novel *Sierro libre de amor* (*The Emancipated Slave of Love*). During the 1430s he entered the Franciscan order. In 1441 he took his first vows as a priest while in Rome and in 1442 his final vows after he had journeyed to Jerusalem. He returned then to Spain, founding a convent at Erbón, where he died in 1450. The convent still stands, a monument to his Galician nationalism, for he believed that Rome, Jerusalem, and Galicia (all of which he had visited) were the three holiest shrines in Christendom.[35]

35. Martin S. Gilderman, *Juan Rodríguez de la Cámara* (Boston, 1977), 13–15.

When the courtly love tradition, which developed in France and is epit-omized in Guillaume de Lorris's portion of *The Romance of the Rose*, made its way into Spain in the 1300s it came into conflict with the idea of male superiority—as indeed had also occurred in France, where it was officially condemned before 1300 by Étienne Champier, the bishop of Paris. At least part of the courtly love ideology involves a female who is socially superior to her male lover. The ideology reflects to some degree a social situation in which women are left behind to rule their estates or principalities by hus-bands who have gone away to fight in the Crusades. Rodríguez was one of these unequal lovers, though in his writing he refused to accept the inequal-ity of his male heroes. The result was that in both his early poems and in his later prose writings death was the inevitable outcome of the attempt to make equal those who were socially unequal.[36] In his poetry and prose Rodríguez suffers a great deal over his unrequited love, but he resolutely refuses to ac-cept a subordinate role for himself in the courtly love relationship. His reso-lution of his dilemma was to seek immortality as a martyr for love.[37]

In light of his personal history, the *Triumph of Women* is a highly ambiva-lent text. He argues not for the equality but for the superiority of women. The treatise opens with a discussion of honor. The discussion turns to the question of whether men or women are the more excellent. Rodríguez retires to a fountain to ponder the question alone and begins to rehearse out loud arguments that could be brought against women, intending to weigh as well arguments in their favor. But in the midst of his accusations the tearful voice of the nymph Cardiano, turned into a fountain for love of Eliso, complains of his words against women, which reflect those of Boccaccio (in the *Corbaccio*). She offers him fifty reasons—based on experience and fact, to which exam-ples of illustrious women of the past are subordinate—for the superiority of women over men.

The tone is combative throughout. Arguments commonly made against women are cited only to be refuted. Agrippa will later use the same strategy,

36. In "The Story of Two Lovers" embedded in *The Emancipated Slave of Love*, death is the only resolution the lovers can find. Ardanlier, the young prince, flees with his love, Liessa, because both families are against the match. After seven years, during which Ardanlier gains fame as a warrior, his father decides to search for him. He discovers Ardanlier's dogs who lead him to Liessa. Accusing her of stealing his son, he draws his sword and kills her and her unborn child. When Ardanlier learns what has happened, he takes his own life. Suicide of the lovers becomes a stock theme in the Spanish sentimental novel thereafter.

Rodríguez consciously modeled himself on the most renowned of the Spanish troubadour poets, Macías (fl. 1350–69), who had actually been a "martyr for love," murdered by the husband of the woman with whom he fell in love.

37. My interpretation follows that of Gilderman, *Juan Rodríguez de la Cámara*, chaps. 2–6.

turning misogynist arguments on their head and using them in favor of women. Thus, Rodríguez turns in favor of women the contention that women are vain in their love of clothes and cosmetics by arguing that they are fond of beautiful things because they are more akin to divine beauty. Women are cleaner than men because they are made of a more purified flesh. The traditional argument that Eve is responsible for original sin is turned around to make Adam responsible, Eve sinning out of ignorance; and this leads to the ingenious conclusion that Christ took the form of a man not because man is superior to woman but because it was man who needed redeeming. Moreover, Christ came into the world through a woman, not a man; he appeared first to women after his resurrection. Still further, all heresies have been invented by men; indeed, most of the criminals of the world have been men, so that if you subtract the number of evil men from the total number of men, it is no surprise that the total number of good women far surpasses the number of good men. Some (it is not clear how many) of these arguments appear in other, earlier, sources. But to my knowledge they had never been brought together in a defense of this kind. The many parallels between Rodríguez's arguments and those of Agrippa are pointed out in the notes to the translation. That the arguments appear in virtually the same order in the two treatises strongly suggests Agrippa's use of this text.

Rodríguez's treatise was quickly recognized as the most compelling of the innumerable defenses of women (most, it seems, in poems) to appear in Spain during the fifteenth century. Fernand de Lucena, the Portuguese nobleman who translated it into French,[38] had come to the court of Philip the Good, duke of Burgundy (1419–67), on the occasion of Philip's marriage to Isabella of Portugal. Martin Le Franc's *Le Champion des dames* (*The Champion of Women*) was composed between 1440 and 1442 for the same Philip the Good who held "the name of love in dutiful reverence," an ironic tribute to a man who had (successively) three wives, thirty known mistresses, and, besides a lawful son and heir, sixteen known bastards!

Martin Le Franc has as his avowed object to defend women against their many detractors and principally against Jean de Meun's contributions to *The Romance of the Rose.* Like his immediate predecessor Rodríguez, Le Franc does not speak directly but in a dream in which the Castle of Love is assaulted by

---

38. The translation, *Triomphe des Dames*, was completed in 1459/1460 and published in French either just before the end of the fifteenth century or just after the beginning of the sixteenth. Hence, it would have been available to Agrippa in printed form. The French translation was published in a collection of Rodríguez's works in Spanish during the nineteenth century: *Obras de Juan Rodríguez de la Cámara (ó del Padrón)* (Madrid, 1884), 381–27 (Spanish text), 319–68 (French translation).

Malebouche (Evil Mouth) and defended by Franc-Vouloir. Their knightly contest takes the form of a debate. The clerics of the universities are all present, together with knights, ladies, and a number of allegorical figures. Before their contest concludes twenty-thousand verses divided into five books have been spoken by personages on both sides. Book 1 speaks of the power of Love; it is the lieutenant of God, governor of the world. Malebouche, fearing that he is losing, calls in another of his advocates, Vilain-Penser (Villainous Thought). Book 2 becomes a catalogue of the entire tradition of misogyny, beginning with the guilt of Eve and including the stories of David, Solomon, Samson, Virgil, Hercules, Aristotle, and other victims of feminine duplicity. Invectives against marriage are included as well, followed by examples of contemporary marriages. The legendary Pope Joan is mentioned, and woman's vanity, jealousy, and rapacity are further exposed. Franc-Vouloir responds in book 3 that both reason and history prove men to be more full of folly than women. Many stories are recited (none of them alluded to by Agrippa) and Jean de Meun is taken to task for his vile language. The lieutenants of Malebouche now having been defeated, there follows in book 4 a list of famous ladies: Judith, Thamaris Queen of the Amazons, the Queen of Sheba, Hortensia, Joan of Arc, the woman who nursed her mother in prison, and others whose exploits prove the superiority of women. In book 5 Franc-Vouloir begins a canticle in honor of the Holy Virgin. The ladies Prudence, Force, Justice, Faith, Hope, Charity, Humility, in company with Virginity, Mercy, and Perseverance, sing successively the praises of the Virgin Mary, who represents woman in all her perfection. At this point a statue of Truth comes to life, condemns the womanhaters, and crowns Franc-Vouloir "champion des dames" with green laurel. The earth bursts open and swallows the whole army of the opponents of woman. At that explosion the poet awakens to versify his dream.

Le Franc's book was published in 1485 in Lyon, twenty-five years after the introduction of the printing press into France; it was published again in 1530. Agrippa may have known it in its earliest printed edition, though the spirit of his work is very different from that of Le Franc. Le Franc rehearses all the stock misognynist views and, moreover, casts his work in the form of allegory common to the Middle Ages (emulating *The Romance of the Rose,* the most popular work of this kind); it is foreign to the rhetorical humanism of Agrippa. There were, however, a number of direct imitations of Le Franc.[39]

---

39. Abel Lefranc has enumerated a number of these, nearly all of which date from the second half of the fifteenth century. See Lefranc, *Grands écrivains française de la renaissance* (Paris, 1914),

On the humanist side of the equation Agrippa may have been familiar not only with Boccaccio's catalogue of famous women but with another by Jacopo Filippo Foresti, *De plurimis claris selectisque mulierebus* (*Concerning Many Famous and Select Women*), published in 1497 and again in 1521. Boccaccio had discussed primarily pagan women, but Foresti includes Christian martyrs and virgins as well in his 184 chapters. Both Boccaccio and Foresti reveal that the *querelle* is gaining momentum.

An Italian humanist treatise very close to Agrippa's in organization and tone is Bartolomeo Goggio's *De laudibus mulierum* (*In Praise of Women*, ca. 1487). It is a long work in seven books, dedicated to Eleanora, wife of Ercole I d'Este, duke of Ferrara. In book 1 he argues in various ways that women have no natural inferiority to men. He argues (as does Agrippa) that women and men were both created with body and soul, so that they do not differ in what is essential. But then, also like Agrippa, he goes on to show that in some important respects the sexes differ and that these differences prove the superiority of women. He cites the commonplace that Adam was created outside Paradise, Eve within it; and he later adds that Eve was created from a more noble matter than Adam (both arguments used by Agrippa, though he uses others as well). Goggio then argues, as does Agrippa, that women are superior by virtue of their physical beauty, because of which they are also intellectually superior to men. In books 2–5 he turns from arguments to examples—the catalogue of famous women from the past—showing that women discovered letters, laws, the arts. Book 5 is a paean to the Virgin Mary, present also in Agrippa. In books 6 and 7 he argues that even though Eve was guilty of the fall, the incarnation has overcome this (as Christine de Pizan argued), but he also adds that there have been no evil results from the fall; whatever has resulted has been because of the normal actions of human nature, implying (but not stating) that the fallen state is our natural state.[40] Although Goggio's treatise is similar in argument to that of Agrippa, he is unlikely to have known it, since it exists in only one (derivative) manuscript copy at the British Library and has never been published. It is important, however, in revealing

---

255–60. Some of these texts have been published in *Recueil des poèsies françoises des quinzième et seizième siècles*, ed. Anatole de Montaiglon and James de Rothschild, 13 vols. (Paris, 1855–78). It is unlikely that Agrippa had read or even knew of these works. That, however, is yet to be demonstrated. In any case, they reveal, as does the proliferation of works during the same period in Spanish, the emergence on new ground of the *querelle des femmes* during the fifteenth century.

40. In this account I have followed the analysis of Conor Fahy, "Three Early Renaissance Treatises on Women," *Italian Studies* 11 (1956) 11–16.

interest in the theme, and the relation of such interest to the patronage of wealthy women.

Another Italian treatise, Maria Equicola's *De mulieribus* (*On Women*, written in 1500 or 1501), was published in 1501 and dedicated to Margherita Cantelma of Mantua, Italy, who employed Equicola as a secretary between 1498 and 1502. The theme of this brief work (sixteen pages) is that men and women are equal, apart from certain physical differences. If they are not in fact equal that is due to custom, which has prevented women from playing more than a secondary role. In an astonishing passage Equicola writes:

> Since this is the case no one with a sane mind will deny that violence, authority, power, and tyranny have been employed against divine law and the laws of nature; and the result has been that the natural freedom of woman has either been prohibited by laws or demolished by custom, at every point absolutely extinguished, abolished, extirpated. The reason is that the lives [of men and women] are turned in different directions. The woman is occupied exclusively at home where she grows feeble from leisure, she is not permitted to occupy her mind with anything other than needle and thread . . . ; then scarcely having passed puberty, authority [over her] is given to a husband; he erects and elevates himself a little more highly [than his wife], he puts her in a household as in a workhouse, [treating her] as if she were unable to grasp the most important matters and hold the higher offices . . . so that just as to the victorious go those conquered by war, in the same way the mind of even the most spirited of women yields to habit. We cannot ignore the fact that we do not exist by natural necessity but that we form into groups either by example and private discipline or by chance and favorable circumstance or even through all these.[41]

Agrippa's peroration seems to be dependent on this passage from Equicola's work.

---

41. Quod si nunc secus est, violentia contra divinum ius naturaeque leges regna, imperia et tyrannidem exerceri sanae mentis negabit nemo; et sic illa feminis naturalis libertas aut legibus interdicta aut consuetudine intercisa, usuque absoluta restinguitur aboletur extirpatur: cum vivendi diversa sit ratio: domi femina detinetur ubi ocio marcescit nec quicquam aliud mente concipere permittitur quam acus et filum . . . ; mox vix annos pubertatis excedens in mariti datur arbitrium, et si paulo altius se erigit et actollit, velut summae rerum altioris provinciae non capax, oeconomicae dedicatur quasi ergastulo . . . ut bello victi victoribus sic virili muliebris cedit animus consuetudine; quam non naturali necessitate constare, sed vel exemplo et disciplina privata vel fortuna et occasione quadam, aut etiam ex his omnibus congregari non ignoramus. The text is cited by Fahy, "Three Early Renaissance Treatises on Women," 38–39 n. 27, who was the first to suggest Agrippa's dependence on it. The translation is mine.

In 1525 Galeazzo Flavio Capra (latinized form Capella) published his *Della eccellenza e dignità delle donne* (*On the Excellence and Dignity of Women*).[42] As its recent editor has noted, it has been ignored for four centuries because of the publication of Castiglione's *Courtier* in 1528, book 3 of which completely overshadowed Capra. His theme is not the superiority but the "dignity" of women, a topos important in fifteenth-century Italian humanism.[43] His discussion is organized around the virtues, theological (faith, hope, love) and classical (justice, temperance, courage, prudence/wisdom). Within this framework, very different from Agrippa's, he illustrates the dignity or excellence of women through examples of famous women, and though he draws from the usual sources, he also uses a number that are foreign to Agrippa. The differences between the two make it doubtful that Capra read Agrippa in manuscript or that Agrippa read and modified his own work after the publication of Capra's treatise. But the two writers illustrate equally well the state of the *querelle des femmes* in the early sixteenth century.

Among French humanists, Agrippa may well have met Symphorien Champier (1472/75–1539), like himself a physician, while in France.[44] Champier's *La nef des dames vertueuses* (*The Ship of Virtuous Women*, 1503, republished in 1515 and 1531 and never thereafter), was, in his lifetime, one of the most popular of his voluminous writings.[45] Champier's view of women, how-

---

42. The work has recently been critically edited by Maria Luisa Doglio (Rome, 1988); her introduction discusses the history of the misogynistic tradition.

43. See the translation, n. 63.

44. Nauert (22–24) reaches this conclusion on the grounds that both were active in introducing Italian ideas into France, that both later became members of the faculty of the University of Pavia in Italy at the same time (1515), and that Champier's works were published along with the texts of Hermes Trismegistus and others in the edition Agrippa must have used. He suggests also that there are traces in Champier's thought of Agrippa's peculiarly ambivalent attitude toward magic and the powers of human reason. As Champier's principal modern biographer has emphasized, however, Champier was nothing if not eclectic in his borrowing—and even copying—from the works of others (Brian Copenhaver, *Symphorien Champier*). Copenhaver surmises that if Champier had not actually met Agrippa earlier, he is likely to have done so in 1524 when Agrippa joined the royal court in Lyon; both moved in the same circle of physicians and humanists. "In the *Galeni historiales campi* (1532), Champier describes a scholarly meeting he once attended in Lyon where one of the disputants was '*Agrippa germano viro multiscio*'. This was probably the famous occultist, and it may also be that the *Clarocampensis* who appears in Agrippa's letters is Champier" (74–75).

45. The work is divided into four books: Praises of Women, Marriage, Prophecy of the Sibyls, and the Book of True Love. Book 1 depends heavily on Boccaccio, whom Agrippa also used.

Book 4, together with a letter to André Briau, has recently been critically edited: *Le livre de vraye amour*, ed. James B. Wadsworth (The Hague, 1962). Wadsworth writes that "the four books of the *Nef des dames* have never been reprinted since 1531 and, though they are not without interest, the first three probably do not merit this honor. The fourth book, the *Livre de vraye amour*, deserves to be better known and better understood" (13). His judgment on the fourth book is

ever, is wholly traditional, which is to say misogynist.[46] Although book 4 of
The Ship of Virtuous Women is regarded as an important contribution to the introduction of Ficinian Neoplatonism into France,[47] Champier's discussions
of women in the other three books—praises of women, marriage,
prophecy—contributed nothing at all to the literature of the defense of
women. Champier illustrates, by contrast, the radical nature of Agrippa's declamation.

It is clear that Agrippa was familiar with both the courtly love and humanist traditions related to the *querelle des femmes*. We can be fairly certain that
he used some texts belonging to each of these traditions; about others we
cannot pronounce one way or another, though they illustrate similar concerns, sometimes even use the same arguments.

In this, as in other respects, Agrippa was something of a weather vane in
his time. He was sensitive to many currents of change taking place around
him: to Luther's fideism, to an emergent skepticism accompanying and in
part independent of it, to the various criticisms of Aristotelian scholasticism,
to the resurgence of Neoplatonism. The same was certainly true of the
woman question, which must have appealed as well to his own maverick tendencies to "prove the opposite," to see his culture with eyes different from
most of his fellows, an attitude which, whatever grief it caused him in the

---

related to the important relation of that text to Ficinian Neoplatonism, of which it was the first
exposition in French.

46. Wadsworth writes: The *"Livre de vraye amour* is generally adjudged feminist, and an episode in
the long-continued *Querelle des femmes*. Again this position requires careful definition. The work is
dedicated to a very noble lady, the daughter of Louis XI, and on that score, must have been
intended as favorable to the ladies. Yet we perceive that the story which illustrates feminine
constancy (Artemisia) is the shortest and the poorest; that in the Boccaccio stories [*Decameron*
5.1, 10.8] the ladies play a passive, subordinate role; and that in the Lucilia fable, the damsel
serves as an example of 'faulse amour'. We note that no attempt has been made to adapt Ficino's
description of reciprocal love to man and woman. Even in his closing paragraphs, where he
apostrophizes his readers, Champier appeals to men and women alike; not until the end does he
make an effort to address a feminine audience: though unable to resist a remark on lascivious
young women, he warns the ladies against predatory males whose fair appearance conceals their
inner corruption. How imbued Champier was with medieval misogyny may be further realized
from the sources of the imagery in which these warnings are made: they are the words of the
preacher and the cleric condemning the lures of feminine beauty turned by Champier against
the male sex" (32).
   I agree wholly with this judgment. The letter to Briau and *The Book of True Love*, though they
both speak of divine and human love, leave virtually unmentioned the love of man and woman,
let alone the reciprocity of love as Champier seeks to promote it in the love or friendship between men.

47. On the latter, see Copenhaver, *Symphorien Champier*, 49–50; Wadsworth, *Le Livre de vraye
amour*, 27–35.

search for position and financial security during his lifetime, makes him an extraordinarily important figure in the history of "the other voice."

Although we can say little with great confidence about Agrippa's debt to other writers, we can say a great deal more about the debt of subsequent writers to him. His declamation was quickly translated from the Latin in which it was written and delivered into French (1530), German (1540), English (1542), Italian (1544), and Polish (1575).[48] Not only was it translated, but the translations were also augmented, usually by additions. Although I have carried out no systematic analysis of changes made in Agrippa's text by translators into various vernacular languages, I have discovered that the German translator added examples to those Agrippa cited, especially from German history. James Turner has found that in the English translations of Agrippa "that of 1542 is a straightforward translation; those of 1652 (one in prose and one in verse) are fervent and sincere arguments on behalf of women; that of 1670 is an expression of 'wit' and social banter, with many added reassurances of playfulness."[49] Some translators also omitted passages, especially Agrippa's discussions of Roman law, which perhaps seemed too abstruse for their intended audience. The French editors of the critical edi-

---

48. *Déclamation de la noblesse et préexcellence du sex féminin*, translated by Louis Vivant, was published by Galliot du Pré, who, in the same year, also reissued Martin Le Franc's *Le Champion des Dames*. The translation was reissued by François Juste at Lyon in 1537. A verse adaptation was made by Banny de Liesse (François Habert) in Paris, 1541, dedicated to the Duchess d'Etampes. Yet another translation was published in Paris by J. Poupy in 1578. One or the other of these translations was reissued in 1686, 1713, and 1726.

Vom Adel und Fürtreffen weibliches Geschlechts, translated by J. Heroldt, was republished in 1566, 1650, 1736, and 1852 and has recently been edited with a commentary by Jörg Jungmayr in the *Archiv für philosophie- und theologiegeschichtliche Frauenforschung* 4 (1988): 53–96.

Of the Nobilitie and Excellencie of Womankynde, translated by David Clapam and published in London, 1542. Clapam's prose translation was turned into heroic couplets by Hugh Crompton in *The Glory of Women; or a Looking-glasse for Ladies*, published in 1652. Another translation, by Edward Fleetwood, *The Glory of Women: or, a Treatise declaring the excellency and preheminence of women above men*, was also published in 1652. An independent translation from Latin, *Female Pre-eminence, or the Dignity and Excellency of that Sex above the Male*, made by Henry Care, was published in London in 1670. Finally, an anonymous translation from French, *On the Superiority of Woman Over Man* was published in New York in 1873.

Della nobiltà et eccellenza delle donne, nuovamente dalla lingua francese nella italiana tradotto, as the title says, was translated from the French translation and not from the Latin. The translation is attributed to Francesco Coccio and was published by Gabriel Giolito (Venice) in 1544. Another version of Agrippa's treatise into Italian, by Alessandro Piccolomini or Lodovico Domenichi, was published in 1545 and 1549 (also in Venice).

49. James Turner, *One Flesh*, 110 and n. 24, n. 26.

tion of Agrippa's declamation have included in the text a passage that circulated in a French manuscript; though they include it in the text, it has all the earmarks of an addition by another hand, and I have placed it in a note.[50] It is clear that the tradition of "borrowing" from Agrippa began with manipulations of his text as it appeared in languages other than Latin.

It is not an exaggeration to say that Agrippa's declamation exercised an influence in the continuing *querelle des femmes* similar to that exercised by Erasmus on humanism and Luther on the Reformation. During the following century and more, texts on this subject proliferated, and many if not most of them counted Agrippa as an immediate source.[51]

In Italy Agrippa's influence spread rapidly through the work of Lodovico Domenichi. Domenichi may have translated Agrippa's declamation into Italian. He certainly wrote *La nobiltà delle donne* (*The Nobility of Women*), published in Venice in 1549. The latter was a plagiarized version of Capra and Agrippa, to whose work he gives wide circulation by presenting it in Italian. From Domenichi arguments in Agrippa such as the etymology of Adam (earth) and Eve (life)—important for the rehabilitation of Eve—are recapitulated by Ortensio Lando (1545), Girolamo Ruscelli (1552), Mutio Manfredi (1575), Tommaso Garzoni (1586), and Lucrezia Marinella (1600).

Agrippa's influence spread with equal rapidity in France. M. A. Screech has demonstrated the direct influence of Agrippa on François de Billon's *Le Fort inexpugnable de l'honneur du sexe femenin* (*The Indestructible Strength of Women's Honor*, 1555).[52] Marc Angenot surveys many texts written in France between 1400 and 1800 and then draws together the themes that run through all of them. Most of the arguments drawn from Genesis are traceable to Agrippa, as are many of the other scriptural arguments.[53] But so also were arguments

50. See the translation, n. 123.

51. The best general bibliography is Ruth Kelso, *Doctrine for the Lady of the Renaissance* (Urbana, Ill., 1956), 326–424. On French texts see Marc Angenot, *Les Champions des Femmes; Examen du discours sur supériorité des femmes 1400–1800* (Montreal, 1977), 173–86; Ian Maclean, *Woman Triumphant: Woman in French Literature 1610–1652* (Oxford, 1977), 271–305. On English texts see Linda Woodbridge, *Women and the English Renaissance: Literature and the Nature of Womankind* (Urbana, Ill., 1986), 329–43; and Nancy Isenberg, "Encomio e vituperio: un secolo e mezzo di scritti inglesi sulla donna (1484–1640)," in *Trasgressione tragica e norma domestica*, ed. Vanna Gentili (Rome, 1983), 92–124. On Italian texts see Conor Fahy, "Three Early Renaissance Treatises on Women," 47–55; and Francine Daenens, "Superiore perche inferiore: Il parodoso della superiorità della donna in alcuni trattati italiani del cinquecento," in *Trasgressione tragica e norma domestica*, ed. Vanna Gentili (Rome, 1983), 41–50.

52. M. A. Screech, "Rabelais, de Billon, and Erasmus: A Re-examination of Rabelais's Attitude to Women," *Bibliothèque d'Humanisme et Renaissance* 13 (1951), 247–49.

53. Marc Angenot, *Les champions des femmes*, 101ff. On the dependence of French writers on Agrippa's interpretation of Gen. 1–3, see Emile Telle, *L'Oeuvre de Marguerite D'Angoulême reine de Navarre*

related to the physical advantages of woman, the role of woman in generation, the beauty of woman, her moral virtues, her modesty, her chastity, her
intellect (especially her eloquence in speaking), political talent (the rule of
women), and warrior virtues. Agrippa does not treat the education of women
except to say that they have been denied it. Turning the argument into a brief
for the education of women was characteristic of writers—both male and
female—in the seventeenth century.

In England Agrippa proved an equally fertile text. Sir Thomas Elyot's
Defence of Good Women (1540), one of the earliest texts in the English *querelle*,
was indebted to the Latin edition of Agrippa, which was accessible to Elyot.
Robert Vaughan (1542) was indebted to Elyot and through him to Agrippa.
Edward Gosnhyll's attack and defense of women (1542) are responses to
Elyot and Vaughan.[54] Agrippa is thus central to the English debate and the
only writer (apart from Castiglione, whose *Courtier* was translated into English in 1561) to recognize that the real issue was not the literary game of
illustrious women and virtues and vices but rather the social problem of the
treatment of women.

TWENTIETH-CENTURY INTERPRETATIONS OF AGRIPPA

Emile Telle wrote in 1937 that Agrippa's treatise "is ignored by everyone today, even our suffragettes."[55] Telle's discussion did not change that situation,
for no one picked up his lead until the 1970s. Since then, however, social and
intellectual historians of early modern Europe intent on recovering the history of women have found Agrippa's declamation squarely in their path.
What have they thought about it? Telle himself believed that Agrippa was
not simply defending women but demonstrating a paradox in an age that
reveled in paradox—a view shared by several more recent interpreters. The
spirit of revolt was in the air, Telle exclaims; the most striking instance of that
spirit in Agrippa is his interpretation of Scripture to the advantage of women.
"Never before 1509 had anyone seen from defenders of the fair sex such a

et la querelle des femmes (Toulouse, 1937), 43–68; and Ian Maclean, *Woman Triumphant: Feminism in French Literature, 1610–1652* (Oxford, 1977), 25–26.

54. See Nancy Isenberg, "Encomio e vituperio: Un secolo e mezzo di scritti inglesi sulla donna
(1484–1640)," in *Trasgressione tragica e norma domestica*, ed. Vanna Gentili (Rome, 1983), 51–124;
and Linda Woodbridge, *Women and the English Renaissance*, 44–45.

55. Telle, *L'Oeuvre de Marguerite D'Angoulême*, 53.

usage of Holy Scripture."[56] In other respects, Telle believes, Agrippa was simply adapting the earlier work of Juan Rodríguez del Padron.

Marc Angenot rejects Telle's perception that Agrippa was simply adapting the earlier work of Rodríguez. His biblical critique is more audacious and his examples come from his own reading and experience. The woman, he says, is for Agrippa "endowed with mysterious powers."[57] Angenot seems to credit the depiction of Agrippa in Bayle's *Dictionary* (1697) as the "grand magician," though he points out that in all his works Agrippa is paradoxical, contradictory, and heterodox. His importance lies in the fact that he "fixes for a long time the plan to follow: theological proofs drawn from Genesis and scriptural, natural, physical, physiological, and psychological proofs drawn from ancient authorities and from 'observation.'"[58]

Ian Maclean cites Agrippa's treatise as among those designed primarily to amuse its readers rather than to persuade, as, he believes, is fairly obviously the case in most antifeminist works.[59] In a later book he adds another note, namely, that even though Agrippa may be called a feminist writer it would be a mistake to regard him as advocating a change in woman's position in society "whose institutions are divinely ordained."[60] But he also includes Agrippa in his more general conclusion that "one way of escaping from the infrastructure of scholastic thought would . . . appear to be by the use of humor. This would explain why contemporary thinkers take texts seriously which are clearly signposted as flippant, or which actually advertise their flippancy: the *Disputatio nova contra mulieres* [*New Disputation Against Women*], Erasmus's *Praise of Folly*, Scaliger's *Exercitationes* [*Exercises*]."[61]

56. Ibid. My translation. This judgment is corroborated in part by John Calvin's criticism of Agrippa on this score in *Traité des scandales* (1550).

57. Marc Angenot, *Les champions des femmes*, 30.

58. Ibid., my translation.

59. Maclean, *Woman Triumphant*, 25–26. The same point is made in a more recent French history of women in the Renaissance that does not analyze Agrippa's treatise but presupposes it as background: Berriot-Salvadore, *Les Femmes dans la société française de la Renaissance* (Geneva, 1990), 51.

Maclean calls attention to the passage in which Agrippa "points out the essentially specious nature of his own feminist composition" (38). He does so again in *The Renaissance Notion of Woman*, 91, though he goes on to say: "it would be unwise to assume that there is nothing but flippancy in the writer's purpose, even if the genre as a whole was intended to amuse rather than persuade."

60. Maclean, *Renaissance Notion of Woman*, 56. Agrippa did not treat institutions as divinely ordained and, as we have seen, said on more than one occasion that they are human creations and so based on custom. But while he challenged institutions intellectually, he did not advocate their overthrow, even when others (e.g., the Protestant reformers) were doing so (while, to be sure, claiming that they were not doing what they were doing).

61. Ibid., 86.

Linda Woodbridge sees Agrippa's oration in relation to the Renaissance tradition of paradox, which she treats more fully than Telle. She believes that much of what Agrippa said was spoken in the spirit of jest. As examples Woodbridge cites his re-creation of woman as a separate species exempt from original sin[62] and such evidence as the greater privacy of women's sexual parts, her hair, which hides those parts and thus renders her more modest, the absence of baldness in the highest part of human anatomy (the head), and others.[63] But all this does not mean Agrippa lacked seriousness. On the contrary, Woodbridge follows Rosalie Colie in treating the oration as rhetorical paradox, and paradoxical literature from Erasmus's *Praise of Folly* (1511) to Montaigne's *Apology* (1575) "exhibits serious intent: the need for such outlandish arguments to maintain an extreme opinion is meant to reflect on the outlandishness of the argument that would be necessary to maintain the opposite extreme."[64] Agrippa's praise of women is "a graphic demonstration of the absurdities one must resort to if one claims superiority for either sex."[65]

Some of his arguments, moreover, are not at all fantastic but the basis for modern feminism; for example, his ringing conclusion that women are forbidden to hold office, plead cases at law, be guardians or tutors, or preach God's word places him "head and shoulders above his contemporaries as a realist in the study of sexual politics."[66] Woodbridge cites with affirmation Agrippa's challenge to the "natural order" and his claim that what exists is based on custom rather than on nature. "Agrippa's lists of great women in history take on new meaning: women have done more in the past than they are doing now, because contemporary society denies them the education and the legal rights they must have to perform what they are capable of."[67] Agrippa saw that the real problem was not literary but social and in doing so "he stood virtually alone." Did Agrippa mean it? She is inclined to believe he did: "One sometimes senses authorial 'sincerity' in controversialist works, as I do with Agrippa; such impressions may frequently be wrong. But whatever the author's personal attitude toward women, it remains clear that the formal

62. Woodbridge, *Women and the English Renaissance*, 40. Agrippa did not actually exempt woman from original sin; he made Adam rather than Eve responsible for it; both, however, were subject to its consequences, though again (reversing tradition) he says those consequences were heavier on Adam than on Eve. But none of this exempts Eve from original sin.

63. Woodbridge points out (ibid., 41) that a later translator (1670) of Agrippa's oration into English, Henry Care, regarded it as an elaborate jest. See also above, n. 47 and related text.

64. Ibid., 41–42, quotation 42. See Rosalie A. Colie, *Paradoxia Epidemica: The Renaissance Tradition of Paradox* (Princeton, 1966).

65. Woodbridge, *Women and the English Renaissance*, 42.

66. Ibid., 43.

67. Ibid.

controversy, for all its preoccupation with stylistic finesse, could occasionally produce a thinker capable of laying philosophic foundations for modern feminism."[68]

Constance Jordan finds the meaning of Agrippa's treatise in a significant shift she sees taking place during the Renaissance, namely, the separation of sex (biology) from social roles.[69] Agrippa's argument follows Genesis 1, in which there is no spiritual distinction between male and female and their physical differences are secondary in importance. Now if women are the equals of men in what matters, then their current disfranchisement has to do with cultural practice rather than natural law. Agrippa shows in his concluding peroration that women were not disfranchised in the ancient world but empowered. Jordan writes that "the decisive determinant of a woman's equality is her economic power, which Agrippa links to her ownership and management of common marital property, and defines according to what he claims are Roman practices following the *ius gentium* [law of nations]."[70] Thus, he makes men and women equal in economic status and argues that "the general practice of denying woman economic and political equality is illegal. In his eyes, woman could perform any kind of public office, execute any kind of public charge."[71] Many writers took this historicist position in the second half of the century in England, thus challenging the universality of the patriarchal model and introducing another, androgynous, one. "Beyond sex and sexual difference, and more important than anything they determine, Renaissance feminists represent men and women as sharing gendered attributes, particularly with respect to the work they do: both labor and often at the same tasks."[72]

The paradox is certainly there, and the arguments generated by it are of uneven value. But the power of Agrippa's declamation lay precisely in his use of argument to reverse the entire misogynistic tradition. This reversal might have been amusing to some—because so utterly fantastic in conception—but its consequences were serious and seriously intended. That Agrippa did not intend to change social structures is true, but no one did—not for the poor, the disfranchised, or women—before the eighteenth century. Maclean is correct in pointing out that Agrippa did not suggest a social revolution. But

68. Ibid., 44.

69. Margaret King makes the same point in *Women of the Renaissance* (Chicago, 1991), 182, though she does not pursue the implications of her observation as fully as does Jordan.

70. Constance Jordan, *Renaissance Feminism: Literary Texts and Political Models* (Ithaca, N.Y., 1990), 123.

71. Ibid., 125.

72. Ibid., 20–21.

he is wrong in asserting that this was so because Agrippa believed social institutions were eternal. Agrippa considered nothing eternal except God in His mystical hiddenness. All else is changeable, reversible. Woodbridge and Jordan, by contrast, plausibly emphasize Agrippa's challenge to the social order on the ground that things can be viewed one way just as well as they can another. Jordan interprets Agrippa in terms more contemporary with us in his denial of the misogynist claim that sex is destiny. Agrippa, like Christine de Pizan and no others before them, refused to treat woman as property (or, as we would say today, solely as sexual objects). It is a telling reflection on our own age that this treatise, written almost five hundred years ago, contains a message that still needs to be heard in contemporary society. I would wager that its claims can still generate a lively debate in a college classroom.

SUGGESTIONS FOR FURTHER READING

The following bibliography is suggestive rather than exhaustive, intended to aid the interested student in pursuing related texts; for that reason it is confined to works in English.

Primary Works

Agrippa, Henry Cornelius (1486–1535). *The Commendation of Matrimony.* Trans. David Clapam. London, 1534.

————. *Of the Vanitie and Uncertaintie of Artes and Sciences.* Edited Catherine M. Dunn. Northridge, CA: California State University, 1974.

————. *The Philosophy of Natural Magic.* Trans. J. F. London, 1651. Repr. Kila, MT: Kessinger Publishing Company, n.d. *The Philosophy of Natural Magic,* same book as above. An early English translation of *De occulta philosophia,* book 1.

Alberti, Leon Battista (1404–1472). *The Family in Renaissance Florence.* Trans. Renée Neu Watkins. Columbia, SC: University of South Carolina Press, 1969.

Ariosto, Ludovico (1474–1533). *Orlando Furioso.* Trans. Barbara Reynolds. 2 volumes. New York: Penguin, 1975–77.

Astell, Mary (1666–1731). *The First English Feminist: Reflections on Marriage and Other Writings.* Ed. and Introd. Bridget Hill. New York: St. Martin's Press, 1986.

Barbaro, Francesco (1390–1454). *On Wifely Duties.* Trans. Bejamin Kohl in Kohl and R. G. Witt, eds., *The Earthly Republic.* Philadelphia: University of Pennsylvania Press, 1976, 179–228. Translation of the Preface and Book 2.

Boccaccio, Giovanni (1313–1375). *Concerning Famous Women.* Trans. Guido A. Guarino. New Brunswick, NJ: Rutgers University Press, 1963.

————. *Corbaccio or The Labyrinth of Love.* Trans. Anthony K. Cassell. Second revised edition Binghamton, NY: Medieval and Renaissance Texts and Studies, 1993.

Bruni, Leonardo (1370–1444). "On the Study of Literature (1405) to Lady Battista Malatesta of Montefeltro," in *The Humanism of Leonardo Bruni: Selected Texts.* Trans. and

Introd. Gordon Griffiths, James Hankins, and David Thompson. Binghamton, N.Y.: Medieval and Renaissance Texts and Studies, 1987, 240–51.

Castiglione, Baldassare (1478–1529). *The Book of the Courtier*. Trans. George Bull. New York: Penguin, 1967.

Elyot, Thomas (1490–1546). *Defence of Good Women: The Feminist Controversy of the Renaissance*. Facsimile Reproductions, Ed. Diane Bornstein. New York: Delmar, 1980.

Erasmus, Desiderius (1467–1536). *The Praise of Folly*. Trans. with an introduction and commentary by Clarence H. Miller. New Haven, CT: Yale University Press, 1979. Best edition, since it indicates additions to the text between 1511 and 1516.

————. *Erasmus on Women*. Ed. Erika Rummel. Toronto: University of Toronto Press, 1996.

Henderson, Katherine Usher and Barbara F. McManus, editors. *Half Humankind: Contexts and Texts of the Controversy about Women in England, 1540–1640*. Urbana, IL: University of Illinois Press, 1985.

Kempe, Margery (1373–1439). *The Book of Margery Kempe*. Trans. Barry Windeatt. New York: Viking Penguin, 1986.

King, Margaret L., and Albert Rabil, Jr., eds. *Her Immaculate Hand: Selected Works By and About the Women Humanists of Quattrocento Italy*. Binghamton, N.Y.: Medieval and Renaissance Texts and Studies, 1983; 2nd revised paperback edition, 1991.

Klein, Joan Larsen, ed. *Daughters, Wives, and Widows: Writings by Men about Women and Marriage in England, 1500–1640*. Urbana, IL: University of Illinois Press, 1992.

Knox, John (1505–1572). *The Political Writings of John Knox: The First Blast of the Trumpet Against the Monstrous Regiment of Women and Other Selected Works*. Ed. Marvin A. Breslow. Washington: Folger Shakespeare Library, 1985.

Kors, Alan C., and Edward Peters, eds. *Witchcraft in Europe, 1100–1700: A Documentary History*. Philadelphia: University of Pennsylvania Press, 1972.

Krämer, Heinrich and Jacob Sprenger. *Malleus Maleficarum* (ca. 1487). Trans. Montague Summers. London: The Pushkin Press, 1928; reprinted New York: Dover, 1971. The "Hammer of Witches," a convenient source for all the misogynistic commonplaces on the eve of the sixteenth century, and an important text in the witch craze of the following centuries.

de Lorris, William, and Jean de Meun. *The Romance of the Rose*. Trans. Charles Dahlbert. Princeton: Princeton University Press, 1971; repr. University Press of New England, 1983.

Marguerite Angoulême, Queen of Navarre (1492–1549). *The Heptameron*. Trans. P. A. Chilton. New York: Viking Penguin, 1984.

Marlowe, Christopher (1564–1593). *The Complete Plays*. Ed. and Trans. J. B. Steane. New York: Viking Penguin, 1969 and often reprinted.

de Pizan, Christine (1365–1431). *The Book of the City of Ladies*. Trans. Earl Jeffrey Richards. Foreword Marina Warner. New York: Persea Books, 1982.

————. *The Treasure of the City of Ladies*. Trans. Sarah Lawson. New York: Viking Penguin, 1985. Also trans. and Introd. Charity Cannon Willard. Ed. and Introd. Madeleine P. Cosman.

Rabelais, François (1494–1553). *Gargantua and Pantagruel.* Trans. J. M. Cohen. Baltimore, MD: Penguin Books, 1955 and numerous reprints. Especially book 3.

Spenser, Edmund (1552–1599). *The Faerie Queene.* Ed. Thomas P. Roche, Jr., with the assistance of C. Patrick O'Donnell, Jr. New Haven: Yale University Press, 1978.

Teresa of Avila, Saint (1515–1582). *The Life of Saint Teresa of Avila by Herself.* Trans. J. M. Cohen. New York: Viking Penguin, 1957.

Vives, Juan Luis (1492–1540). *The Instruction of the Christian Woman.* Trans. Rycharde Hyrde. London, 1524, 1557.

Weyer, Johann (1515–1588). *Witches, Devils and Doctors in the Renaissance: Johann Weyer, De praestigiis daemonum.* Ed. George Mora with Benjamin G. Kohl, Erik Midelfort, and Helen Bacon. Trans. John Shea. Binghamton, N.Y.: Medieval and Renaissance texts and Studies, 1991.

Wilson, Katharina M., ed. *Medieval Women Writers.* Athens, GA: University of Georgia Press, 1984.

———. *Women Writers of the Renaissance and Reformation.* Athens, GA: University of Georgia Press, 1987.

Wilson, Katharina M. and Frank J. Warnke, eds. *Women Writers of the Seventeenth Century.* Athens, GA: University of Georgia Press, 1989.

Women Writers in English 1350–1850 (series). 30 volumes projected; 8 published through 1995. New York: Oxford University Press.

Secondary Works

Beilin, Elaine V. *Redeeming Eve: Women Writers of the English Renaissance.* Princeton: Princeton University Press, 1987.

Benson, Pamela Joseph. *The Invention of Renaissance Women: The Challenge of Female Independence in the Literature and Thought of Italy and England.* University Park, PA: Pennsylvania State University Press, 1992.

Bietenholz, Peter G. and Thomas B. Deutscher, editors. *Contemporaries of Erasmus: A Biographical Register of the Renaissance and Reformation.* 3 volumes. Toronto: University of Toronto Press, 1986.

Bloch, R. Howard. *Medieval Misogyny and the Invention of Western Romantic Love.* Chicago: University of Chicago Press, 1991.

Clark, Elizabeth A. *Ascetic Piety and Women's Faith: Essays on Late Ancient Christianity.* Lewiston, NY: Edwin Mellen Press, 1986.

Colie, Rosalie A. *Paradoxia Epidemica: The Renaissance Tradition of Paradox.* Princeton: Princeton University Press, 1966.

Copenhaver, Brian. *Symphorien Champier and the Reception of the Occultist Tradition in Renaissance France.* The Hague: Martinus Nijhoff, 1978.

Davis, Natalie Zemon. *Society and Culture in Early Modern France.* Stanford: Stanford University Press, 1975. Especially chapters 3 and 5.

Dixon, Suzanne. *The Roman Family.* Baltimore: Johns Hopkins University Press, 1992.

Fahy, Conor. "Three Early Renaissance Treatises on Women," *Italian Studies*, 11 (1956): 30–55. On pp. 47–55 Fahy lists treatises on the equality or superiority of women written or published in Italy during the fifteenth and sixteenth centuries.

Ferguson, Margaret W., Maureen Quilligan, and Nancy J. Vickers, eds. *Rewriting the Renaissance: The Discourses of Sexual Difference in Early Modern Europe.* Chicago: University of Chicago Press, 1987.

Gardner, Jane F. *Women in Roman Law and Society.* Bloomington, IN: Indiana University Press, 1986.

Gilderman, Martin S. *Juan Rodríguez de la Camara.* Boston: Twayne Publishers, 1977.

Herlihy, David. "Did Women Have a Renaissance? A Reconsideration," *Medievalia et Humanistica*, NS 13 (1985): 1–22.

A History of Women in the West

    Volume 1: *From Ancient Goddesses to Christian Saints.* Ed. Pauline Schmitt Pantel. Cambridge, MA: Harvard University Press, 1992.

    Volume 2: *Silences of the Middle Ages.* Ed. Christiane Klapisch-Zuber. Cambridge: Harvard University Press, 1992.

    Volume 3: *Renaissance and Enlightenment Paradoxes.* Ed. Natalie Zemon Davis and Arlette Farge. Cambridge: Harvard University Press, 1993.

Horowitz, Maryanne Cline. "Aristotle and Woman," *Journal of the History of Biology*, 9 (1976): 183–213.

Hull, Suzanne W. *Chaste, Silent and Obedient: English Books for Women, 1475–1640.* San Marino, CA: The Huntington Library, 1982.

Jordan, Constance. *Renaissance Feminism: Literary Texts and Political Models.* Ithaca: Cornell University Press, 1990.

Keefer, Michael H. "Agrippa's Dilemma: Hermetic 'Rebirth' and the Ambivalences of *De vanitate* and *De occulta philosophia*," *Renaissance Quarterly*, 41 (1988): 614–53.

Kelly, Joan. "Did Women Have a Renaissance?" in her *Women, History and Theory.* Chicago: University of Chicago Press, 1984. Also in Renate Bridenthal, Claudia Koonz, and Susan M. Stuard, *Becoming Visible: Women in European History.* 2nd ed. Boston: Houghton Mifflin, 1987), 175–202.

———. "Early Feminist Theory and the *Querelle des Femmes*," in *Women, History and Theory.*

Kelso, Ruth. *Doctrine for the Lady of the Renaissance.* Foreword by Katharine M. Rogers. Urbana, IL: University of Illinois Press, 1956, 1978.

King, Margaret L. *Women of the Renaissance.* Foreword by Catharine R. Stimpson. Chicago: University of Chicago Press, 1991.

Laqueur, Thomas. *Making Sex: Body and Gender from the Greeks to Freud.* Cambridge, MA: Harvard Univeristy Press, 1990.

Lerner, Gerda. *Creation of Feminist Consciousness, 1000–1870.* New York: Oxford University Press, 1994.

———. *The Creation of Patriarchy.* New York: Oxford University Press, 1986.

Lochrie, Karma. *Margery Kempe and Translations of the Flesh.* Philadelphia: University of Pennsylvania Press, 1992.

Maclean, Ian. *The Renaissance Notion of Women: A Study of the Fortunes of Scholasticism and*

Medical Science in European Intellectual Life. Cambridge: Cambridge University Press, 1980.

———. *Woman Triumphant: Feminism in French Literature, 1610–1652.* Oxford: Clarendon Press, 1977.

Matter, E. Ann and John Coakley, eds. *Creative Women in Medieval and Early Modern Italy.* Philadelphia: University of Pennsylvania Press, 1994. (sequel to the Monson collection, immediately below)

Matulka, Barbara. *The Novels of Juan de Flores and Their European Diffusion: A Study in Comparative Literature.* New York: Institute of French Studies, 1931.

Monson, Craig A., ed. *The Crannied Wall: Women, Religion, and the Arts in Early Modern Europe.* Ann Arbor: University of Michigan Press, 1992.

Nauert, Charles G., Jr. *Agrippa and the Crisis of Renaissance Thought.* Urbana: University of Illinois Press, 1965.

Okin, Susan Moller. *Women in Western Political Thought.* Princeton: Princeton University Press, 1979.

Pagels, Elaine. *Adam, Eve and the Serpent.* New York: HarperCollins, 1988.

Pomeroy, Sarah B. *Goddesses, Whores, Wives, and Slaves: Women in Classical Antiquity.* New York: Schocken Books, 1976.

Rose, Mary Beth, ed. *Women in the Middle Ages and the Renaissance: Literary and Historical Perspectives.* Syracuse: Syracuse University Press, 1986.

Schmitz, R. "Agrippa, H. C." *Dictionary of Scientific Biography.* Ed. C. C. Gillispie, et al. (New York, 1970–80), 1:79–81.

Screech, M. A. "Rabelais, de Billon and Erasmus: (A Re-examination of Rabelais's Attitude to Women)," *Bibliothèque d'Humanisme et Renaissance,* 13 (1951): 241–65.

Sommerville, Margaret R. *Sex and Subjection: Attitudes to Women in Early-Modern Society.* London: Arnold, 1995.

Stuard, Susan M., "The Dominion of Gender: Women's Fortunes in the High Middle Ages," in Renate Bridental, Claudia Koonz, and Susan M. Stuard, eds., *Becoming Visible: Women in European History.* 2nd ed. Boston: Houghton Mifflin, 1987), 153–72.

Tetel, Marcel. *Marguerite de Navarre's Heptameron: Themes, Language & Structure.* Durham, NC: Duke University Press, 1973.

Treggiari, Susan. *Roman Marriage: Iusti Coniuges From the Time of Cicero to the Time of Ulpian.* Oxford: Oxford University Press, 1991.

Walsh, William T. *St. Teresa of Avila: A Biography.* Rockford, IL: TAN Books & Publications, 1987.

Warner, Marina. *Alone of All Her Sex: The Myth and the Cult of the Virgin Mary.* New York: Knopf, 1976.

Wiesner, Merry E. *Women and Gender in Early Modern Europe.* Cambridge: Cambridge University Press, 1993.

Willard, Charity Cannon. *Christine de Pizan: Her Life and Works.* New York: Persea Books, 1984.

Wilson, Katharina, ed. *An Encyclopedia of Continental Women Writers.* New York: Garland, 1991.

DECLAMATION ON
THE NOBILITY AND PREEMINENCE
OF THE FEMALE SEX

Henricus Cornelius Agrippa

To the Very Illustrious Lord Maximilian of Transylvania, Councillor of the Emperor Charles V,[1] Henricus Cornelius Agrippa sends his greetings

Some twenty years have elapsed, illustrious Maximilian, since, having been appointed lecturer at the University of Dôle, Burgundy, I explained, to the admiration of all and in honor of our exalted princess Margaret [of Austria],[2] the book On the Marvelous Word by John Reuchlin,[3] and, as an introductory lecture, delivered a notable encomium in praise of her.[4] At that time several of the important men of the city—among others Simon Verner (Vernerius), dean of the church of Dôle and

1. Maximilian Transilvanus was a councillor involved in matters of trade, in 1523 with the imperial cities and in 1534 with the Netherlands and the North Sea city of Lübeck. See Karl Brandi, *The Emperor Charles V: The Growth and Destiny of a Man and of a World-Empire*, trans. C. V. Wedgwood (Atlantic Highlands, N.J., 1939), 187, 355. Thus, in 1529, the year in which Agrippa addressed this letter to him, Maximilian appears to have been a councillor specializing in economic matters. He may thus also have been involved in matters of patronage.

2. Margaret of Austria (1480–1530) was the daughter of the future emperor Maximilian (1459–1519, emperor 1493–1519). Twice married and widowed by 1504, she refused marriage thereafter, focusing her energies on raising her nieces and nephew (the future Charles V, emperor 1519–55) and ruling the Netherlands. She patronized many learned men, of whom Agrippa was one. On her see Alice Tobriner and IG [sic], "Margaret of Austria," in Peter G. Bietenholz and Thomas B. Deutscher, eds., *Contemporaries of Erasmus: A Biographical Register of the Renaissance and Reformation*, 3 vols. (Toronto, 1985–87), 2:389–90, and sources cited.

3. Johann Reuchlin (1454/5–1522) was one of the most renowned of German humanists. Educated in Greek and Hebrew, as well as in Latin, he was the first Christian to produce a Hebrew dictionary, *De rudimentis hebraicis* (*Basic Principles of the Hebrew Language*, 1506). His kabbalistic dialogues *De verbo mirifico* (*On the Marvelous Word*, 1494) and *De arte cabalistica* (*The Practices of the Kabbalah*, 1517) were based on his study of Hebrew. See Heinz Scheible, "Johann Reuchlin," in Bietenholz and Deutscher, eds., *Contemporaries of Erasmus*, 3:145–50, and sources cited.

4. It is very likely that Agrippa's essay on women and his lectures on Reuchlin circulated in manuscript, especially in France, where at least one version published in that country contained additions to Agrippa's text by another hand. See n. 123.

vice chancellor of the university,[5] *whom you know well—vigorously urged me to dedicate some writing to the aforementioned princess. All of them urged me with incessant requests, pressed me in their letters, and repeated that by such a work I would gain no inconsiderable favor with this princess. I consented, thinking it wrong to reject the persistent entreaties of such great men and to despise the prospect of favor of so great a princess. I then chose as a subject for the work "The Nobility and Preeminence of the Female Sex," thinking it appropriate that I should consecrate and dedicate it to that princess who, more than all the illustrious women of our age, seems to be a unique paragon of the nobility and excellence of women. For with her as a protector and a witness, this little book would gain considerable authority against those whose sole occupation is to censure women. That I did not fulfill my vow to her Highness at that time was not owing to the distance between us or the fleetingness of time or inconstancy on my part or a change of purpose, nor even to the difficulty of the subject or my lack of talent, but to the calumnies of a certain Catilinet. (What kind of calumny it was you will be able to see from my actual complaint to him, which I sent you with this material).*[6] *Overwhelmed and full of indignation at his hypocrisy, I suppressed the book, keeping it secret until now, and I have chosen not to use this occasion to kill two birds with one stone,*[7] *even if it were worth the effort, for I was confident that someone could be found who would help me present the book to my lady.*

And so, having now returned to this country, I have judged it proper to keep my word and, without delaying any longer, to offer to our princess this book which is in all justice due to her, as much by my bond as by my promise. She will perceive that during this time I have never forgotten her, that I have not broken any oath, and that the baseness of others has not prevailed over the steadfastness of my own heart, which is thoroughly devoted to her virtues and her praises.

And if now your wisdom does not reject my project, I will see to it that this book is published together with several others of my works, although I see how slight the subject is and rendered without elegance of expression. But I wish this little book, written earlier in my youth, revised only in a few places as you see in this exemplar sent to you in haste, to be offered to this princess in the same form today as it was earlier (as is the manner of speaking among those called canonists), even to the prejudice of my reputation. But being older now, I shall compose works on more profound and more serious topics, which will be more elevated and worthier of her Highness. I would not wish the princess to judge my talents on the basis of these trifles of my youth,[8] *for, if she wished, my talents could be of use to her in even the greatest matters in peace and in war.*

5. I have found no additional information about this person.

6. Jean Catilinet was provincial superior of the Franciscans in Burgundy. His attack on Agrippa is discussed in the introduction.

7. Literally, "utilize this pot of lime to whiten two walls." See Cicero, *Familiar Letters*, 7.29.2.

8. The idea that this declamation was a trifle is suggested by Agrippa also in his *Apologia adversus*

So, then, lest anyone, through pride, through presumption of knowledge, full of contempt for my insignificance, malevolent toward my talent, may come to despise, calumniate, slander, or tear apart my work, I commend it to your majesty to be defended and protected together with the splendor of feminine nobility, and also the glory of womanly excellence. And I hope that I shall readily be granted pardon for having defended the superiority of women over men, since it is for such a noble princess that I have written this book and at the urging and protection of your lordship that I have published it. Farewell. Antwerp, April 16, 1529. I await your judgment.

To the Divine Margaret Augusta, Very Merciful Ruler of Austria and Burgundy, Henricus Cornelius Agrippa sends his greetings

I have undertaken—as boldly as I can but not without shame—to treat a topic previously ignored but by no means far from the truth, namely, the nobility and preeminence of the female sex. I confess that more than once, within myself, my boldness has struggled with my sense of shame. For on the one hand, I thought it the height of ambition and boldness to seek to enumerate in a discourse the innumerable merits of women, their virtues, and their complete superiority. On the other hand, to accord women preeminence over men seemed the height of shame, almost the sign of an emasculated spirit. This is perhaps the reason very few have attempted to set forth in writing the praises of women and no one I know of has yet dared to affirm their superiority over men.[9] *But I thought it would be the height of ingratitude and a*

---

calumnias propter declamationem de vanitate scientiarum, chap. 42: "Proinde declamatio non judicat, non dogmatizat sed que declamationis conditiones sunt, alia joco, alia serio, alia false, alia saevere dicit: aliquando mea, aliquando aliorum sententia loquitur, quaedam vera, quaedam falsa, quaedam dubia pronunciat. . . .Nec omni loco animi mei sententiam declarat. . . .Multa invalida argumenta adducit." (A declamation does not judge or dogmatize; rather the conditions of a declamation are that it speaks at various times playfully, seriously, falsely, with fury. . . .Sometimes the opinions offered are mine, sometimes those of others. Some things declared are true, others false or doubtful. Not in every place is the opinion declared my own. . . .Many of the arguments brought forward are invalid.) The Latin passage is cited by M. A. Screech, "Rabelais, de Billon, and Erasmus: A Re-examination of Rabelais's Attitude to Women," *Bibliothèque d'humanisme et Renaissance* 13 (1951): 246 (my translation).

It is worth noting that Agrippa said the same in defending *Vanity* against attacks in the same *Apologia*. "At every turn, Agrippa excused himself by saying, 'I was only declaiming,' and by charging that his accusers were so slow-witted that they took all his statements seriously" (Nauert, 196). Nauert goes on to add, however, that even in cases where it is obvious that Agrippa is joking, "the jokes reflect his own state of mind."

9. As my introduction points out, at least three others had made this argument prior to Agrippa: Juan Rodríguez del Padron, Bartolomeo Goggio, and Maria Equicola. Agrippa certainly knew the work of Rodríguez and quite possibly that of Equicola. Still, as the introduction also points out, Agrippa *was* original in important respects.

sacrilege to begrudge in silence the genuine praises owed so worthy a sex, and to snatch them away, so that the sex is defrauded of its merits and its glory by suppression of the known truth. I vacillated anxiously, caught between diverse and contradictory attitudes, but my powerful fear of ingratitude and sacrilege triumphed over my sense of shame and gave me the boldness to write this treatise, since I feared appearing more bold if I kept silent. I regarded it, indeed, as a happy omen that Heaven had reserved and assigned to me a task that seemed until now to have been totally neglected by the multitude of scholars.

I shall therefore proclaim the glory of woman; I shall not conceal her honor,[10] and I am far from embarrassed at introducing such a subject. And far from being ashamed of the subject I have taken up (since I would think that if I rank women above men I shall certainly be criticized for it), I am sure that I shall scarcely be excused for taking up so sublime a topic in so modest a style—were it not that the constraint of time, the difficulty of the subject, and the justness of the case protect me, and also the fact that I undertook this task with no interest in flattery or adulation. I have no great desire to dress up praise with pretentious images or charming fictions, but only to present my thesis based on reason, authority, examples, and evidence drawn from Holy Scripture and both civil and canon law.

It is to you, most serene Margaret, that I have dedicated my work. The five gods Apollo, Diana, Day, Dawn, and Vulcan[11] have glorified none of the outstanding women of this generation throughout the entire world as much as they have glorified you in nobility of birth, preeminence of virtues, glory of deeds. You, who have reached the pinnacle of virtue, who surpass by your life and manners all the praises that are proclaimed about the merits of the female sex, are the living example and exemplary witness of virtue. To you, therefore, I offer this work in order that, like the sun, you may cause to shine all the more brilliantly the honor and glory of this sex that is yours. Fare most fortunately and well, you who are absolute perfection—the noblest of noble women and the honor, adornment, and glory of princesses.

---

10. The verbs "proclaim . . . conceal" echo Ps. 40:10 (Vulgate 39:9–11) and Prov. 12:23.

11. It is not at all clear why Agrippa has put together these five gods/goddesses. Apollo and Diana (= Greek Artemis) were twins; there is at least one story that relates them to Vulcan (= Greek Hephaistos). Day and Dawn are personifications of light; there are stories about Dawn in Greek mythology, only one mention of Day in Hesiod and no stories so far as I know.

Day may be a corruption for Dis, God of the underworld. With this emendation, the list involves deities who each bring a particular gift to womankind: Apollo music, Diana chastity, Dis gems and gold (from the underworld), Aurora youth, and Vulcan finely wrought jewelry. I owe this suggestion to an anonymous reader.

L. Beliaquetus[12]

Cease, inane babbler, to praise the male sex
more than is just, lest you build a worthless heap of
encomia.
Cease, if you are wise, to condemn the female sex with
malicious words that lack reason.
If you weigh each sex carefully in your balance, whoever
is male will yield to the female sex.
But if you hesitate to believe this, and the issue seems
still unsettled to you,
I have here a witness who has not appeared
elsewhere,
a short work which studious Agrippa has recently
compiled,
Praising the female sex as superior to the male.

EQUALITY OF SOUL IN
MEN AND WOMEN

God most beneficent,[13] Father and creator of all good things, who alone possesses the fecundity of the two sexes, created humans in his image, male and female created he them.[14] Sexual distinction consists only in the different location of the parts of the body for which procreation required diversity. But he has attributed to both man and woman an identical soul, which sexual difference does not at all affect. Woman has been allotted the same intelligence, reason, and power of speech as man and tends to the same end he does, that is, [eternal] happiness, where there will be no restriction by sex. For according to the truth of the gospel, although all will return to life in their own sex, they will no longer carry out the functions of their sex, but it has been promised to them that they will be similar to angels.[15] Thus, there is no preeminence of nobility of one sex over the other by reason of the nature of the soul; rather, inwardly free, each is equal in dignity.

---

12. This poem belongs to the published edition of Agrippa's declamation (as "recently brought to light" makes clear) and was not part of the lecture he delivered. It may have been written by Agrippa (and so may be self-praise or disguised self-praise) or by the person named at its beginning, otherwise unknown to me. The poem serves as a kind of advertisement, announcing the content and extolling the diligence of its author.

13. The Latin phrase is "Deus Optimus Maximus"; it is based on the common appellation "Jupiter Optimus Maximus" and means literally "highest [and] best."

14. Gen. 1:26.

15. See Mark 12:25 and parallels: Matt. 22:30 and Luke 20:35–36.

But, setting aside the divine essence of the soul in humans, in everything else that constitutes human being the illustrious feminine stock is almost infinitely superior to the ill-bred masculine race. This will appear indisputable when I have demonstrated it (and this is my purpose), not by forged or counterfeit speech or by the snares of logic in which many sophists love to entrap us, but by taking for authorities the best authors and by appealing to authentic historical accounts, clear explanations, the evidence of Holy Scripture, and prescriptions drawn from the two laws.

THE SUPERIORITY OF WOMEN IN THE CREATED ORDER

So let me begin my subject at the beginning. Woman was created as much superior to man as the name she has received is superior to his. For Adam means earth, but Eve is translated as life.[16] And as far as life is to be ranked above earth, so far is woman to be ranked above man.

There is no reason to say that passing judgment on things from their names is a weak argument. We know in fact that the Sovereign Creator of things and of their names knew the things before naming them, and He, since He could not be deceived, has fashioned the names[17] in such a way that He expressed the nature, propriety, and usage of things. Indeed, as Roman laws also attest, truth consists in the conformity of ancient names with things; indeed, names are a manifest signification of the things named.[18] Therefore, theologians and lawyers consider the argument based on names

---

16. Jerome, in his *Liber de nominibus Hebraicis* (*Book of Hebrew Names*), says Adam means "humus, vel terra, sive terrena" (soil, especially earth, or earthly); Eve means "calamitas, aut vae, vel vita" (calamity, either woe or life) *PL*, 23:819, 822, respectively. If Agrippa was using Jerome as a source here, he conveniently omitted the tenor of what Jerome had to say about Eve— characteristic of his treatment of the patristic, as of the biblical and classical traditions.

17. Agrippa bases this theory of the divine imposition of names on Genesis (see 2:19–20; 5:2) and develops it in his *On Occult Philosophy*, bk. 1, chap. 70, "De virtute propriorum nominum" (Of the Virtue of Proper Names). There he argues that each name Adam gave to animals or things signified something and the animal or thing had the power of the thing(s) signified. The signifying power, he continues, comes from two sources: the influence of celestial harmony (natural) and the imposition of man (arbitrary); when both these significations meet in any voice or name, then that name has a double virtue that makes the name efficacious enough to act as often as it is uttered at the right time and place. As an example he cites the holy rites of the Romans before they besieged a city; they inquired of the true name of it and the name of the god under whose protection it was; then they called forth the gods that protected the city, cursing the inhabitants so that their gods would leave and the Romans could conquer.

18. One Roman law pertaining to women is illustrative: *Institutes*, 2.7, De donationibus ("Concerning Gifts"), 3. It deals with gifts after marriage which were still called *ante nuptias* by Justinian,

to carry great weight. We read, for example, in reference to Nabal: "Thus as his name indicates, he is a fool and foolishness is with him."[19] And for the same reason Paul, in his letter to the Hebrews, wishing to place in evidence the excellence of Christ, has recourse to the following argument: "He has become as much superior to the angels as the name he has received as a heritage is superior to theirs."[20] And in another passage: "He has given to him a name that is above every name, that at the name of Jesus every knee should bow in heaven, on the earth, and under the earth."[21]

Add to this that the great power of canon and civil law rests in the connections, meanings, agreements, and demonstrations of words,[22] in subsid-

---

and in a passage that echoes the point Agrippa is making in the text, Justinian's successors wrote: "We, desiring to provide rules in the most perfect manner, and wishing names to bear some relation to things, have decreed that donations of this description may not only be increased but may be instituted during marriage, and that they shall not be called *ante nuptias* but *propter nuptias*, and be classed with dowries in this respect, and that just as dowries can not only be increased but also created during marriage, so gifts of this kind introduced 'on account of marriage' may not only antedate the ceremony, but may also be increased or originated after it has been performed."

19. 1 Sam. 25:25. The Hebrew word *nabal* means fool.

20. Heb. 1:4.

21. Phil. 2:9–10.

22. The Latin here is: "verborum obligationibus, in verborum significationibus, in conditionibus et demonstrationibus."

Significatio verborum is the title of *Digest*, 50.16, which provides explanations of some 246 terms, both juristic and nonjuristic. The definitions collected from juristic works include almost all classical jurists. The collection was prepared for furthering a better understanding of terms and locutions used in the *Digest*. The title begins with an explanation of the phrase "si quis" = "if anybody," which is interpreted to include both men and women. Two examples dealing with women that illustrate the idea of signification of words: *Digest*, 50.16.46 (Ulpian): "We should understand the expression 'mother of a family' to signify one who does not live unchastely, for the morals of the mother of a family distinguish and separate her from other women. Hence it makes no difference whether she is married or a widow, freeborn or emancipated, as neither marriage nor birth, but good morals constitute the mother of a family" (Scott, 11:266). And *Digest*, 50.16.152 (Gaius): "There is no doubt that both males and females are included under the term 'men'" (Scott, 11:281).

Many *Verborum obligationes* ("Concerning Verbal Obligations," *Digest*, 45.1) are discussed in the *Digest*. Most of these have to do with agreements between men, though a few involve women, for example, 45.1.70 (Ulpian): "A woman who gave a dowry to my compatriot, Glabrio-Isidor, made him promise this dowry to a child if she should die during marriage, which she did. It was decided that an action under the stipulation would not lie, as a person unable to speak could not stipulate" (Scott, 10:111).

Conditionibus et demonstrationibus ("Concerning Testamentary Conditions and Designations, Their Reasons and Their Modifications") is found in *Digest*, 35.1, and elsewhere. Two examples that relate to women: *Digest*, 35.1.9 (Ulpian): "Where a husband bequeathed a legacy to his wife payable when she had children, we are accustomed to say that he did not have in his mind those

iary conditions and discussions of that kind, and in the annotations on the laws, as can be understood in the laws themselves and other comparable sections of canon and civil law. For in law we argue from the interpretation of a name, likewise from the meaning of a word and its composition, and, in addition, from the etymology of a name, from the application of a name, from the order of words. For the two laws wisely weigh the meanings of names in order to make an interpretation based on them.

Cyprian also argued against the Jews that the first man received his name from the four cardinal directions—Anatolie, Dysis, Arctos, Mesembrios— which signify East, West, North, and South.[23] And in the same work, Cyprian interprets the name of Adam to mean "because the earth was made flesh," although such an interpretation is in disagreement with the tradition of Moses, since, in Hebrew, the name is written, not in four letters, but in three.[24] However, let us not criticize the exposition of so holy a man, who did not understand Hebrew. Many hallowed interpreters of Holy Scripture have been ignorant of this language without their having come to grief over it. But even if one cannot agree to give me a similar license and permit me to derive the etymology of the name of Eve in honor of women according to my judgment, one should at least grant my right to say that, according to the mystical symbols of the kabbalists, the name Eve itself has more affinity with the ineffable name of the all-powerful divine *tetragrammaton* than the name Adam, which accords with the name of God neither in letters nor in form nor in number.[25]

We shall abstain from these mysteries for now; they have been read by few, understood by even fewer, and require a much more extended discussion than it is convenient to include here. For the moment we shall search out the

---

children whom his wife already had at the time when he made his will" (Scott, 7:301). And *Digest*, 35.1.22 (Julian): "Whenever a bequest is made to a wife under the condition that she will not marry, and she is charged to deliver the property bequeathed to Titius if she should marry, it has been well established that if she marries she can claim the legacy and will not be compelled to execute the trust" (Scott, 7:305; the original law was enacted in 242 CE and changed as here in the sixth century).

23. These mean, literally, "rising, setting, the Great Bear, and midday" (Cyprian, *De montibus Sina et Sion adversos Judeos*, chap. 4 [*PL*, 4:911–12]). Rodríguez offers the same interpretation of the four cardinal directions as reason 43 for the superiority of women, citing Isidore of Seville rather than Cyprian (246).

24. Cyprian, chap. 4 (*PL*, 4:912B). See the following note.

25. The *tetragrammaton* is the four letters that form the name of God: YHWH. The name of Eve shares two of these letters (HW); Eve is derived from the root "to live" (see Gen. 3:20) and God from the root "to be" (see Exod. 3:13–14), which are the same in Hebrew. The name of Adam (ADM), derived from "earth" (see Gen. 2:7), shares none of the letters of Eve or of God in Hebrew.

excellence of woman, not only according to her name, but according to the facts themselves, her duties, and her merits. For this, let us (as they say) search the Scriptures, and, starting with the beginning of creation itself, let us show what dignity superior to that of man woman has obtained from her place in the order of creation.

We know that, among all that was created by the best and greatest God, the essential difference consists in the fact that certain things live forever, while others are subject to corruption and change,[26] and that, in the course of this creation, God advanced following an order that consisted in beginning with the more noble of the first group and ending with the most noble of the second. Thus, he created first the incorruptible angels, then the souls (for Augustine affirms that the soul of our first parents was created at the same time as the angels, before the body was fashioned).[27] Then he created the incorruptible bodies, such as the heavens and the stars, and elements that, although incorruptible, are nonetheless subject to various changes. And from them he formed all other things that are subject to corruption, proceeding again by ascent, from the more insignificant through all degrees of honor to the perfection of the universe. Thus were created first minerals, then vegetables, plants and trees, followed by animated beings, and finally brute beasts, in order: reptiles, fish, birds, quadrupeds.[28]

And after all this he created two human beings in his image, man first, then woman, in whom the heavens and the earth, and every embellishment of both, are brought to perfection. For when the Creator came to the creation of woman, he rested himself in this creation, thinking that he had nothing more honorable to create; in her were completed and consummated all the wisdom and power of the Creator; after her no creation could be found or imagined. Since, therefore, woman is the ultimate end of creation, the most perfect accomplishment of all the works of God and the perfection of the universe itself, who will deny that she possesses honor surpassing every other creature? Without her the world itself, already perfect to a fault and complete at every level, would have been imperfect; it could only be perfected in the

26. It is a fundamental postulate of Aristotelian physics that the heavens—from the moon outward—are eternal and possessed of a different kind of matter from that of the earth. Only the elements (earth, air, fire, water) from which the earth and things on it are created are corruptible; heavenly matter (a fifth essence) is unchangeable, incorruptible.

27. See Augustine, *De Genesi ad litteram*, 7.22–24; *The Literal Meaning of Genesis*, 2 vols., trans. J. M. Taylor, Ancient Christian Writers 41–42 (New York, 1982), 2:23–26. See also *City of God*, 12.23.

28. Although Agrippa is following the order of creation in Gen. 2, he also has in mind Aristotelian physics (see above, n. 26) and the hierarchical view of the "plenitude of nature" known as the "great chain of being." The classical study of this idea is Arthur Lovejoy, *The Great Chain of Being* (New York, 1936).

creature of all others by far the most perfect. For it is unreasonable and absurd to think that God would have finished so great a work with something imperfect.

Since the world itself has been created by God as a circle of absolute perfection, it is fitting that the circle be perfected by this particle capable of being the link that unites perfectly the beginning of the circle with its end. That is how, at the time of creation, woman was the last in time of all things created; in the conception of the divine mind, however, she was first of all, as much in prestige as in honor, as was written about her by the prophet: "Before the heavens were created, God chose her and chose her first."[29] Indeed, it is a commonplace among philosophers to say (I cite their own words): "The end is always the first in intention and the last in execution."[30] For woman was the last work of God, who introduced her into our world as the queen of a kingdom already prepared for her, adorned and perfect in everything. It is therefore right that every creature love, honor, and respect her; right also that every creature submit to and obey her, for she is the queen of all creatures and their end, perfection, and glory, absolute perfection.[31] This is why Wisdom says of her: "She glorifies her noble birth by living with God, for even the Lord of all has loved her."[32]

How far woman surpasses man in nobility of race by reason of the order in which she was created the sacred word bears witness most abundantly to us. Woman in fact was fashioned with the angels in Paradise, a place absolutely full of nobility and delight, while man was made outside of Paradise in the countryside among brute beasts and then transported to Paradise for the creation of woman.[33] It is for this reason that woman, thanks to a particular

---

29. Ecclus. 24:5, 9. In this passage Wisdom personified (female) is praising herself. See also Prov. 8:22–31. The French editors of the critical edition of Agrippa's text believe that he has in mind the *Shekinah* (female in Hebrew), the tenth and last emanation of God in kabbalistic mysticism, even though he never says so. This passage from Ecclesiasticus, cited by Agrippa, supports that assertion but does not confirm it.

30. Rodríguez cites this as the first reason for the superiority of women (217) and is most likely Agrippa's immediate source. I have been unable to find the statement in Aristotle, from whom it presumably comes.

31. The Latin here is parallel to the concluding line of Agrippa's dedication to Margaret. Martin Le Franc, *Le Champion des dames*, uses almost the same language as Agrippa uses here, suggesting that God surpassed himself in creating Eve after Adam; she was God's "supreme and last work, perfect and sovereign" (Antoine Campaux, *La Questions des femmes au quinzième siècle* [Paris, 1856], 19). The idea that the less noble should serve the more noble is included in Rodríguez's first reason for the superiority of women (218).

32. Wisd. of Sol. 8:3 (Apocrypha).

33. In Gen. 2 Paradise is located "in Eden, in the east" (2:8). God placed Adam in the Garden of Eden (2:15) and it was there that Eve was created (2:18ff.). The idea was already expressed in

gift of nature—as if the particularly eminent place of her creation had accustomed her to it—is not subject to vertigo, nor are her eyes troubled when she looks down from however great a height, although these troubles are frequent among men.[34] Moreover, if a man and a woman are equally in danger of drowning, and if no outside help intervenes, the woman maintains herself longer on the surface of the water, while the man is not long in sinking and heading toward the bottom.[35]

The connections between the nobility of a place and the notoriety of an individual are clearly confirmed by the civil laws and the sacred canons;[36] and custom in every nation[37] pays special attention to assess not only men but also every living being and even every thing, judging that the more honorable their place of origin, the more noble they are. This is why Isaac recommends to his son Jacob not to take a wife from the country of Canaan, but from Mesopotamia in Syria, because they are of a higher status.[38] This same point of view appears in the passage in John where Philip says: "We have found Jesus, son of Joseph of Nazareth." Nathaniel responds to him: "Can anything good come from Nazareth?"[39]

---

medieval texts. Rodríguez offers this as the first reason for the superiority of women (see above, n. 31) and includes with this idea the notion that woman was created from a more perfect matter; the latter is also stated separately as his third reason (217–18). See below, n. 40.

34. Rodríguez says in reason 39 for the superiority of women that when a man goes up he loses his senses but a woman loses nothing. The argument is that man was formed in the lowest sphere, woman in the highest; hence women are more at home in the higher sphere (244–45). What source lies behind both writers I have been unable to determine.

35. Ibid. Rodríguez says (also reason 39) that men, being made from earth, tend to fall to the center of the earth. Women, made of a higher essence (reason 42), do not get seasick as men do and are sustained longer in the water (245).

36. In *Digest*, 21.1, De Aedilicio edicto ("Concerning the Edict of the Aediles"), 31, Quod si nolit ("If the Vendor Refuses"), par. 21, Qui mancipia ("Persons Who Sell Slaves"), the commentator Paul writes: "Persons who sell slaves should always state their nationality at the time of the sale, for very frequently the place of the nativity of a slave either attracts or deters the purchaser, and hence it is to our interest to know in what country he was born; for it is presumed that some slaves are good because they are sprung from a nation which has not an evil reputation, and others are considered to be bad because they are derived from a nation which is rather disreputable than otherwise" (Scott, 5:172).

37. *Omnium gentium consuetudo* (custom of all nations) as used here is close to the definition of natural law in the *Digest*, 1.1.1, par. 3: "Natural law is that which nature teaches to all animals" (Scott, 2:209).

38. Gen. 25:20; 28:2, 6. Genesis says Paddan-aram. This is a region in Mesopotamia near the junction of the Khabur and Euphrates rivers. One of its chief cities was Haran, from which Isaac and Jacob procured wives. "Syria" is an indefinite term but includes, often, Palestine and everything east and north.

39. John 1:45–46.

Let us now go on to other things. Woman is superior to man by reason of the material of her creation, because she was made not from something inanimate, not from vile clay as man was, but from a purified material, endowed with life and soul, I mean a reasonable soul, sharing the divine intelligence. In addition, man has been made by God from the earth, which, according to its own nature, so to speak, produces animals of every kind when the celestial influence cooperates with it. But woman has been created by God alone, outside of every celestial influence and of every spontaneous action of nature, without the contribution of any force, and she is found with an absolute cohesion, complete and perfect. Man lost one rib from which woman, that is, Eve, was formed during the sleep of Adam, a sleep so profound that he did not even feel that the rib God took from him and gave to the woman had even been removed. Thus, man is the work of nature, woman the creation of God.[40] Therefore, woman is generally more capable than man of receiving the divine light with which she is often filled, something one can see even today in her refinement and extraordinary beauty.

THE SUPERIOR BEAUTY OF WOMEN

Since beauty itself is nothing other than the refulgence of the divine countenance and light which is found in things and shines through a beautiful body,[41] women—who reflect the divine—were much more lavishly endowed and furnished with beauty than man.[42] Whence follows the wonder-

---

40. See Gen. 2. This argument was already a commonplace in the Middle Ages. See the introduction.

41. The French editors point out that this is the definition of beauty in the Neoplatonic tradition. Marsilio Ficino (1433–99), the Florentine Platonist philosopher, for example, writes: "The appearance of a man, which because of an interior goodness graciously given him by God, is beautiful to see, frequently shoots a ray of his splendor, through the eyes of those looking at him, into their souls. Drawn by this spark like a fish on a hook, the souls hasten toward the one who is attracting them. This attraction, which is love, since it derives from the beautiful, good, and happy, and is attracted to the same things, we do not hesitate to call Goodness, Beauty, Blessedness, and a God" (*Marsilio Ficino's Commentary on Plato's "Symposium"*, trans. Sears Reynolds Jayne [Columbia, Mo., 1944], sixth speech, chap. 2 [p. 183]). Maclean (16–17) notes that Bonaventura "provides a justification for the contemplation of women, in claiming that through their beauty it is possible to communicate with God," an argument, he notes, reminiscent of Platonism, but rare in scholastic writings.

42. On the characteristics of the physical beauty of women that follow, Agrippa elaborates in *On Occult Philosophy*, 2.27. The French editors suggest that this catalogue of feminine beauty gives us a glimpse of the canons of beauty in poetry and painting inspired by Neoplatonic philosophy at the end of the fifteenth and the beginning of the sixteenth century. They point out that ideas of female beauty and harmony are connected to notions of moral goodness and virtue (e.g., the beauty of her hair, eyes, teeth, etc., is related to light; her symmetry and proportion are

ful softness of the female body to sight and touch, her tender flesh, her fair
and clear complexion, her shiny skin, the beauty of her head decked with
long silky hair shining and supple, the great majesty of her face with its
cheerful demeanor, her face the most fair of all creatures, her neck of a milky
whiteness, her forehead large, high, noble. She has penetrating and sparkling
eyes, which unite with grace and an amiable gaiety; the slender arch of her
eyebrows rises above them, between them a beautiful open space, descend-
ing from which is a nose straight and properly proportioned. Under her nose
is a red mouth, which owes its beauty to the symmetrical disposition of her
tender lips; when she smiles we see her dainty teeth, well placed, as white as
ivory, less numerous however than those of men,[43] for woman is neither a
glutton nor as aggressive as man. The cheeks and jaws impart to her a tender
softness, a tinted rosy glow and modest demeanor; she has a delightful chin,
round and with a charming dimple. Under this she has a slender neck, long
enough, elevated above round shoulders. Her throat is delicate and white, of
medium size. Her voice and her words are agreeable; her chest, large and
prominent, makes for a harmonious unity of flesh and of breasts, with the
same plumpness on each side both in the firmness of the breasts and in the
roundness of both them and the belly. Her sides are supple, her back rises
straight up; she has long arms, her hands are well made, her fingers slender
with fine joints, her hips and thighs full, her calves plump, the ends of her
hands and feet rounded off; all her members are full of vitality. In addition,
she has a modest bearing, propriety in her movement, dignified gestures, and
is, besides, in her whole body of a universally attractive proportion and symmetry, figure, and carriage.

There is no other creature who offers a sight so admirable, a similar marvel to behold, to the point that one would have to be blind not to see that
God himself has put together in woman all that is beautiful in the whole
world. All are dazzled by her beauty and love and venerate her on many accounts, to such an extent that we regularly see incorporeal spirits and demons perish with passionate love for women (and this is not an erroneous
belief but a truth confirmed by many experiences).

---

connected to the circle, the symbol of harmony in Renaissance thought, and language suggesting harmony in this respect appears in connection with a description of her eyebrows, mouth,
stomach, etc.). Although there may be some justice in these comments, several counter observa-
tions are in order: that some of these details are already present in reason 5 offered by Rodríguez
for the superiority of women (218–19), that the idea that female beauty renders women equal to
man was stated by Basil of Caesarea, a prominent Greek church father (*On Virginity*, 17; PG,
30:706), and that moral virtue is explicitly mentioned only in connection with her teeth.

43. On the fewer teeth in women than in men, see Pliny, *Natural History*, 7.16.

I will pass in silence the accounts poets have given us about the loves of the gods and about the women who have loved them—the love of Apollo for Daphne, of Neptune for Salmonea, of Hercules for Hebe, Iole, and Omphale[44]—and about the women loved by other gods, and the particularly numerous loves of Jupiter. But this beauty, a divine gift loved by gods and men, Holy Scripture in many passages celebrates and praises as the supreme grace which has been accorded to women.

Thus, we read in Genesis that the sons of God, seeing the daughters of men, found them beautiful and chose among them wives to their liking.[45] We read also of Sarah, the wife of Abraham, that she was beautiful above all other women of the earth, I shall say even astonishingly beautiful.[46] And when the servant of Abraham saw Rebecca, a maiden of exceptional beauty, he said quietly to himself: "This is the one whom the Lord has destined for Isaac, the son of Abraham."[47] Abigail, wife of Nabal, a very wicked man, was shrewd and wise fully as much as she was beautiful, which permitted her to save the life and goods of her husband from David's rage. This wicked man was saved by the beauty of his wife; David said to her: "Go in peace to your house; behold, I have understood your plea and honored your beauty." For since all beauty is either spiritual, vocal, or corporeal, and since Abigail was beautiful in all three respects inasmuch as she had at once a wise disposition, facility with words, and a beautiful body, she became one of the wives of David following the death of her husband Nabal.[48]

Bathsheba also was so beautiful that David was smitten with love for her, married her after the death of her husband, and elevated her above all others

44. On Apollo and Daphne, see Ovid, *Metamorphoses*, 1.452–566.

Neptune does not love Salmonea but rather Salmonea's daughter, Tyro. See Ovid, *Amores*, 3.6.43; Propertius, 3.19.13.

On Heracles (Hercules) and Hebe, see Homer, *Odyssey*, 11.601–4, where Heracles is married to Hebe. In Ovid, *Metamorphoses*, 9.401–2, Heracles persuades Hebe to make him young again.

On Heracles and Iole, see Ovid, *Metamorphoses*, 9.140; Heracles's rumored passion for Iole was the cause of the jealousy of Heracles's second wife, Deianira. See Boccaccio, *Concerning Famous Women*, chap. 21.

On Heracles and Omphale, see Sophocles, *Women of Trachis*, lines 247ff.; the story is also found in other writers. Omphale was a Lydian queen who purchased Heracles as a slave after Heracles had been told by Apollo that only by selling himself thus could he be cured of his madness (for having killed Iphitus, son of Eurytus, king of Lydia and father of Omphale). Omphale bought him and set him to various labors; according to Ovid's account, Omphale had a son (Lamus) by Heracles (see *Heroides*, 9.53ff.).

45. Gen. 6:2.

46. Gen. 12:14.

47. Gen. 24:14–61, esp. 24:14.

48. 1 Sam. 25 tells the story of David, Nabal, and Abigail. The passage cited is 1 Sam. 25:35.

in honor by making her queen.[49] The Sunamite Abishag, because she was a young girl of very great beauty, was selected to lie down beside King David in order to restore life to the aging king.[50] For this reason the old king wished to elevate her to the highest honors, and after his death she was made all-powerful queen.[51] The same thing resulted from what we read about the marvelous beauty of queen Vashti and about Esther, who was preferred to her and was more striking than Vashti had been in her exceedingly beautiful and lovely face.[52] Of Judith we read also that the Lord increased her beauty to such a degree that those who saw her were struck speechless with admiration.[53] Not to be prolix, there is also Susanna, whose appearance was admirably soft and beautiful.[54] And we read also that Job, after the various temptations and trials he endured, received as a gift from the Lord—in addition to the other things he earned with the greatest patience—three very beautiful daughters, infinitely more charming than the Three Graces, more beautiful than had ever been found anywhere in all the land.[55]

49. The story of David's infatuation and subsequent marriage to Bathsheba is told in 2 Sam. 11–12. The story of David's promise to Bathsheba that her son Solomon would rule after David is told in 1 Kings 1. The text never states that David elevated Bathsheba above all his other wives, but that is implied in the promise that Solomon would become king.

50. 1 Kings 1:1–4. In *The Commendation of Matrimony*, Agrippa writes: "And therefore both to men that be somewhat aged, yea and to those that be decrepit, and in whom there is no might of generation, no hope left of propagation, it is nevertheless lawful to marry, and (if a man may say it) oftentimes necessary, whereby they may pass forth the later days of their life, in the company of their well beloved wife, with more joy, surety, and less care. Whereof David, very old, with the Sunamite maid, is an example" (spelling modernized). Screech, "Rabelais, de Billon, and Erasmus," 260 and n. 3, cites this as an example of antifeminism in Agrippa, since Agrippa is here thinking about the comfort of the old man rather than the well-being of Abishag. However, it might also be argued that Agrippa was rejecting the Greek biological tradition that made all women cold and moist in temperament and all men hot and dry. David and Abishag reverse biological stereotypes here.

51. Adonijah, the son of David who had taken the throne while David was still alive and was subsequently displaced by Solomon (at the command of David), requested of Solomon, through Bathsheba, that he be given Abishag as his wife (1 Kings 2:13–21). Solomon responded by having Adonijah put to death. Thereafter, no further mention is made of Abishag.

52. Esther 1–2.

53. Jud. 8:7. The text states only that "she was beautiful in appearance, and had a very lovely face," but Agrippa embellishes it. Rodríguez, reason 14, makes much of the beauty of Judith and Esther, through which they saved their people (222–23).

54. See Sus., verse 31. Susanna belongs to the Apocrypha of the Hebrew Bible and was one of the stories added to the book of Daniel. In the Septuagint (the Hellenistic Greek translation of the Hebrew Bible) and in the Latin Vulgate, the story of Susanna is added to the book of Daniel as chap. 13. In the Greek text of Theodotion, and in the Old Latin, Coptic, and Arabic versions, the story forms an introduction to the book of Daniel (chap. 1).

55. Job 42:15, which says simply: "And in all the land there were no women so fair as Job's

Let us read, next, the stories of the holy virgins—without doubt we shall marvel to see what astonishing beauty, what admirable grace the Catholic church accords them above all other daughters of men in singing solemnly their praises. But the first among all, and one whose praise should surpass all others, is the Virgin Mary, mother of God, immaculate virgin, whose beauty the sun and moon admire and from whose face so much chastity and holiness of beauty shines forth that even though she dazzles all eyes and all hearts, never did a single mortal man entice her with his inducements or with even the least thought.

If I have spoken at great length in citing almost word for word these passages from the Holy Bible where mention is so often made of beauty, it is in order that we may understand clearly that the beauty of women merits for them an increase in esteem and honor, not only in the eyes of humans, but also in the eyes of God. We read also in another passage of Holy Scripture that God ordered all those of the male sex to be put to death, boys included, but that he spared beautiful women.[56] And in Deuteronomy [21:11] it is granted to the sons of Israel to choose beautiful captives for wives.

THE SUPERIOR VIRTUE OF WOMEN

Beyond her admirable beauty, woman has also been endowed with a dignity of virtue not granted to man. Thus, women grow their hair so long that they are able to conceal the more shameful parts of their bodies. Moreover, it is never necessary for a woman to touch these parts of the body, though it is the usual practice for men to do so. Finally, nature itself has disposed the sexual parts of women according to a marvelous decency, inasmuch as they are not protruding as they are in men but remain internal, concealed in a secret and secure place.[57]

---

daughters." It is probably the appearance of the number 3 in the text that leads Agrippa to compare Job's daughters to the Three Graces.

The Three Graces were Aglaia (Splendor), Euphrosyne (Mirth), and Thalia (Good Cheer). They were daughters of Zeus and Eurynome but were usually treated together, a triple incarnation of grace and beauty, and not as separate personalities. The gods took delight in them when they danced, and the person visited by them was happy. They and their companions, the Nine Muses, were the queens of song (Hesiod, *Theogony*, 35–52, 905–909). Based on a representation of them from antiquity, the Three Graces appear often in Renaissance art, most famously in Botticelli's *Primavera*, painted only a few years before Agrippa wrote this declamation.

56. In Num. 31:17–18 Moses orders that all males be killed together with every woman who has known a man, but that young virgins be spared. Nothing is said about their beauty. See also Exod. 1:16; Deut. 20:14. Rodríguez offers this as reason 45 for the superiority of women (251).

57. Rodríguez includes both these points in reason 14 for the superiority of women (221–22). What source lies behind both writers I have been unable to determine.

In addition, nature has accorded a greater sense of shame to women than to men. For this reason a woman suffering from an abscess in her private parts which places her life in danger has very often chosen to die rather than to be exposed, in the course of her care, to the view and the touch of a surgeon.[58] And this virtue of shame women preserve even at the hour of their death or after their death, as is especially evident in those who die by drowning. According to Pliny, whose authority is confirmed by experience, nature, sparing the modesty of the dead, causes the woman to float face down, while the man remains on his back.[59]

Another argument may be added: the most noble part of the human body, that by which we are different from the brute beasts and by which we judge our nature divine, is the head, and more particularly in the head, the face. But the head of man is disfigured by baldness, while nature accords woman the great privilege of not becoming bald.[60] And besides, men's faces are so often deformed by beards (hateful even to them) and covered with ugly hairs, that they can scarcely be distinguished from beasts. The face of woman, on the contrary, remains always unblemished and beautiful. For this reason the Law of the Twelve Tables cautioned women against scraping their

58. Symphorien Champier (1472/75–1537), a contemporary of Agrippa's and like him both a doctor and a humanist by profession, corroborates this observation, and with approval, in his *Claudii Galeni historiales campi* (Basel, 1532), chap. 40, p. 17. The topos that women would rather die that expose themselves to dishonor is a commonplace among writers in behalf of women.

59. "Men's corpses float on their backs, but women's on their faces, as if nature spared their modesty after death" (Pliny, *Natural History*, 7.17). Maclean writes: "Other arguments about sexual psychology based on physical phenomena are also attacked in the Renaissance; an example is the proof of natural modesty (*verecundia*) in woman—the fact that drowned female corpses float face downwards in the water—which is discredited by Bonacciuoli, and shown to result from purely anatomical causes" (43).

60. Aristotle turns baldness into another advantage for the male: "Thus if we reckon up three points, that the brain itself has but little heat, and further that the skin round it must needs have still less, and again that the hair must have still less than the skin inasmuch as it is the furthest removed from the brain, we should reasonably expect baldness to come about this age upon those who have much semen. And it is for the same reason that the front part of the head alone goes bald in man and that he is the only animal to do so; the front part goes bald because the brain is there, and man is the only animal to go bald because his brain is much the largest and the moistest. Women do not go bald because their nature is like that of children, both alike being incapable of producing seminal secretion. Eunuchs do not become bald, because they change into the female condition. And as to the hair that comes later in life, eunuchs either do not grow it at all, or lose it if they happen to have it, with the exception of the pubic hair; for women also grow that though they have not the other, and this mutilation is a change from the male to the female condition" (*Generation of Animals*, 5.3, 783b32–784a11; Barnes, 1:1,211). Here again Agrippa is turning the Aristotelian tradition on its head.

cheeks, out of fear that a beard might grow on them and conceal their shame.[61]

Without doubt the strongest of all arguments for the neatness and the purity of the woman, the one most evident to all, is that once she has washed herself carefully, every other time she immerses herself in clear water the water shows no trace of impurity. But man, however much he has washed, disturbs and dirties the water again each time he washes himself.[62] Moreover, every month women (following a natural rhythm) discharge from their secret parts superfluous humors that men evacuate continuously from the face, a much more noble part of the human body. In addition, although it must be granted that human beings alone among living creatures turn their faces to heaven,[63] nature and fortune have been so marvelously attentive and so full of regard toward women that, if by chance they fall unexpectedly, they nearly always fall on their backs[64] and seldom or never fall forward on their head or face.

Should we pass over the fact that in the procreation of the human race nature has preferred woman to man? This is particularly evident in the fact that only the female seed (according to the stated opinions of Galen and Avicenna) provides matter and nourishment for the fetus, while that of the man intervenes only a little because it affects the fetus rather as accident to

---

61. Pliny, *Natural History*, 11.58: "Only man has cheeks below the eyes (the old word for cheeks was *genae*, used in the Twelve Tables in the prohibition of women's lacerating them). The cheeks are the seat of modesty: on them a blush is most visible" (LCL, 3:531). Also Cicero, *On the Laws*, 2.23.59: "Women shall not tear their cheeks" (LCL, 16:445). Cicero cites this law as having been derived from Solon and placed in Table Ten (X.4) of the Twelve Tables. The prohibitions cited by Pliny and Cicero are against self-mutilation as a sign of mourning, not against shaving.

Rodríguez, reason 14, has much to say about bodily hair; among his comments is that beards make men's faces less attractive than those of women (222).

62. Rodríguez cites this as reason 6 for the superiority of women and asserts that it is experimentally attested (219). A recent biographer of Juan Rodríguez regards this "proof" as original with him (Gilderman, *Juan Rodríguez de la Cámara*, 110). Angenot, on the other hand, says it is tradition, commenting: "What is most curious is that, transmitted by tradition, we find this notion repeated endlessly by theoreticians on the superiority of women until the eighteenth century" (*Les Champions des femmes*, 18 [my translation]). The "origins" of many of these ideas are extremely difficult to pin down.

63. Ovid, *Metamorphoses*, 1.85–86. Renaissance humanists made much of this classical topos related to the dignity of man. See Charles Trinkaus, *In Our Image and Likeness: Humanity and Divinity in Italian Humanist Thought*, 2 vols. (Chicago, 1970). But Maclean comments: "the enhancement of the dignity of mankind, which is at the centre of humanism, does not seem to affect in any way the low status of women" (*Woman Triumphant*, 22–23).

64. I have been unable to find any source for this assertion.

substance.[65] The greatest and principal task of women, says the law, is to conceive and to protect the fruit of their conception.[66] The reason we see so many sons resemble their mothers is that they have been procreated by her blood. The resemblance is often evident in their physical appearance but is always present in their character: if the mothers are stupid, the sons are stupid; if the mothers are wise, the sons breathe wisdom. It happens otherwise with fathers, who, even if intelligent, very often beget stupid sons or who, stupid themselves, produce wise sons, provided that their mother is wise. This is why mothers love their children more than fathers do, because they recognize and find in them much more of themselves than the fathers do. And this same reason explains why we have by nature, I think, more affection toward our mother than toward our father, to the point that although we esteem our father, it is our mother alone that we love.[67]

Still further, nature has given to woman a milk of such great power that it not only feeds infants but also strengthens the sick and serves as a life support for some adults.[68] Proof of this we read in Valerius Maximus: a young plebeian woman nourished her mother, who was imprisoned and who otherwise would have died of hunger.[69] For this act of piety the mother was released, a

---

65. On the differences between Aristotle and Galen on the question of generation see the introduction.

66. 1 Tim. 2:15: "Yet woman will be saved through bearing children" is the text I believe Agrippa had in mind. Jungmayr (345 n. 70) suggests as a source Cicero, *Pro Cluentio*, 12.33, describing a case in which a large legacy was bequeathed by a dying husband to his pregnant wife on condition that she "take every care that the child she had conceived should come safely to the birth" (LCL, 9:255) and to that end live with her mother-in-law until the child was born. (The text goes on to say that another condition of the bequest was that the wife bear a son; otherwise the money would go to another male member of the family.)

67. The view expressed here is a reversal of that of Thomas Aquinas, who elaborated Aristotle's view that a child loved his father more than his mother, since "the father is principle in a more excellent way than the mother, because he is the active principle, while the mother is a passive and material principle" (*Summa Theologica*, trans. Fathers of the English Dominican Province, 3 vols. [New York, 1947–48], 2:1,302 [II.II, q. 26, a. 10]). Another transformation of tradition by Agrippa.

68. Pliny, *Natural History*, 28.23.

69. Valerius Maximus, *Factorum ac dictorum memorabilium libri IX* (*Nine Books of Memorable Deeds and Sayings*), 5.4.7; Pliny, *Natural History*, 7.36. Both writers say, as does Agrippa, that the prison was thus consecrated as a temple of piety. Boccaccio omits this detail in his retelling of the story: *Concerning Famous Women*, chap. 63.

Valerius Maximus' book is usually referred to simply by the author's name, which will be the practice hereafter in these notes. This book was compiled in 31 CE as a handbook of illustrative examples for rhetoricians drawing on many writers preceding Valerius. His handbook was much used by medieval and Renaissance writers. Agrippa later calls attention to Valerius, along with Plutarch and Boccaccio, as authors on whom he has depended. See n. 201 and related text.

public grant of perpetual food supplies was made to them both, and the prison was consecrated as a temple of piety.

It is, moreover, recognized that the woman nearly always manifests more piety and mercy than the man, and even Aristotle himself asserts that these qualities are characteristic of the female sex.[70] For this reason, I think, Solomon said: "Where there is no woman, a sick man groans,"[71] doubtless because the woman has an adroitness and an astonishing good humor when she aids and assists the sick, or because her milk is the most powerful remedy that can be found at the immediate disposition of the feeble, the sick, and even the dying, for restoring them to life. Hence, as the doctors say, the heat of her breasts placed on the chest of men who are enfeebled by old age, re-vives, augments, and conserves in them their vital heat. David knew it; he chose in his old age the young Sunamite Abishag and was warmed by her embrace.[72]

Moreover, as everyone knows, the woman is readier for the second duty of procreation because she is able to take a man from the age of ten years old or even younger; the man, on the contrary, is unable to beget until later. Moreover, no one can ignore the fact that alone among viviparous creatures, the woman is again inclined to sexual activity after she is pregnant and even not so long after she has delivered.[73] Her organ, called a womb, is so well adapted to conception that a woman, one reads, sometimes has conceived without uniting with a man;[74] the illustrious naturalist has written of a certain woman that she was impregnated with the semen released by a man in a

70. Rodríguez offers this as reason 18 for the superiority of women (227–29). Both he and Agrippa cite Aristotle's *History of Animals*, 9.1, 608a22–27, 608b1–3. These passages are discussed in the introduction.

71. See Ecclus. (Sirach) 36:25: "Where there is no wife, a man will wander about and sigh." Rodríguez offers this as reason 16 for the superiority of women and uses the same quotation from Ecclesiasticus (227).

The sentences immediately following, in which Agrippa attributes extraordinary healing powers to women, are paralleled by a passage in *Of the Vanitie and Uncertaintie of Artes and Sciences*, 310: "The chiefest physicians also confess that they have learned many most excellent remedies of women and worthy to be put in their books, and as it were, singular things left to the poster-ity." And shortly afterward, pointing out the usually harmful effects of medicine, he writes: "an old wife of the country doth more safely cure with a Medicine made with one, or two herbs of the garden, with the work of nature, than that physician with his monstrous and sumptuous receipts made with a doubtful conjecture" (310, spelling modernized).

72. 1 Kings 1:1–4. See n. 50 and related text.

73. Aristotle, *On the Generation of Animals*, 4.5, 773b; Pliny, *Natural History*, 10.83.

74. Plato maintained that the womb was a separate animal, "avid for generating," a view Galen rejected. Agrippa is not here taking the side of Plato, but he may be alluding to it. The idea was controversial during the Renaissance. Rabelais, in the *Tiers livre* (*Third Book*), took the side of Plato. See Screech, *The Rabelaisian Marriage*, chap. 6.

bath.[75] To this can be added another astonishing miracle of nature: that a pregnant woman, if her inclination pushes her in this direction, eats without danger meat that has not been cooked, raw fish, and even often enough charcoal, dirt, rocks; she also, without suffering from it, digests metals, poison, and other similar products and converts them into a salutary nourishment for herself.[76]

No one will be astonished at the number of prodigious phenomena—beyond those I have cited—that nature is pleased to create among women, if he has read the works of philosophers and doctors, of which an example—the only one I shall add—is ready to hand: menstruation. Menstrual blood, in addition to the fact that it cures some quartan fevers, hydrophobia, epilepsy, elephantiasis, depression, madness, and many other similar pernicious illnesses, is not less worthy of being admired for numerous other effects; among other marvels, for example, it extinguishes fires, calms tempests, keeps away the danger of raging waters, expels every nuisance, unbinds spells, and puts evil spirits to flight.[77] There are many other powers that I have no intention of presenting at the moment. However, for good measure, I shall add one more, drawing on the traditions of doctors and philosophers that are supported by experience. This divine gift that women have received and that all admire I wish to call the power of healing themselves of all sorts of illnesses by their own means, without recourse to some foreign or external aid.

But what passes beyond every marvel, and the thing in itself the most miraculous, is that a woman alone, without a man, has been able to beget human beings, a privilege that has not been accorded to a man. The Turks and the Mohammedans do not contest this; they believe in fact that a good number among them have been conceived without male semen (they call

75. Averroës writes: "Et vicina quaedam mea, de cujus sacramento confidere multum bene poteramus, juravit in anima sua quod impraegnata fuerat subito in balneo lavelli aquae calidae, in quo spermatizaverunt mali homines, cum essent balneati in illo balneo" (A certain neighbor of mine, in whose testimony we can place complete trust, swore an oath on her soul that she had been suddenly impregnated while she was washing in a bath of hot water in which evil men had released their sperm while they were bathing in that water) (*Averrois Cordubensis colliget libri VII* [Venice, 1552], 14; my translation). Averroës was apparently the first to cite this example, which was widely repeated. See Claude Thomasset, "The Nature of Woman," 57.

76. See Agrippa, *On Occult Philosophy*, 1.42, De quorundam veneficiorum admirandis virtutibus ("Of the Wonderful Virtues of some Kinds of Sorceries"). See also the following note. The 1542 English translation omits the additional examples that follow and picks up again with the discussion of speech.

77. Agrippa follows Pliny, *Natural History*, 28.23. However, menstrual blood is said by Pliny also to have negative effects, in this passage and more especially in 7.15. Here is another instance in which Agrippa is reversing the tradition.

these beings in their language the Nefesogli), and they tell of islands where women conceive under the influence of a gentle wind, though we do not accept their contentions as true. For only the Virgin Mary, she alone I say, conceived Christ without a man and gave birth to a son of her own substance and through the fecundity of her nature. The blessed Virgin Mary is the true and natural mother of Christ, and Christ himself is the true and natural son of the Virgin Mary. I say "natural" because he is a human being and, besides, the natural son of the Virgin, inasmuch as this Virgin herself was not under subjection to the corruption of nature. As a consequence, she did not give birth in pain, nor was she under the power of a man,[78] and her fecundity was so great from the prior blessing of God that she did not need help from a man in order to conceive. Among brute beasts it has been established that some females are fecund without the participation of the male, as female vultures, an example cited by Origen, who recounts it in his work against Faustus [Celsus].[79] It has also been said of certain mares in antiquity that they conceived under the breeze of Zephyr, as the following lines from a poet of antiquity express it:

> With their mouths open, all stand gathered together on the high rocks facing the west wind; they sniff the light air, and often conceive without being mated, impregnated by the wind.[80]

What shall I say now of speech, the divine gift which more than anything else renders us superior to the beasts—a gift Hermes Trismegistus believes to be as precious as immortality[81] and Hesiod the best treasure of

---

78. See Gen. 3:16; Matt. 1:18.

79. Origen, *Contra Celsum*, I.37. Origen himself refers back to other authors as authorities for the assertion (*Contra Celsum*, trans. Henry Chadwick [Cambridge, 1965], 36 and n. 2). Chadwick cites, among others, Tertullian (*Against the Valentinians*, 101), Plutarch (*Moralia*, 286C), and D'Arcy Thompson, *Glossary of Greek Birds* (1936), 83.

80. Virgil, *Georgics*, 3:273–75. There was a male fear that "if there were a female sperm with an active and formative capacity [which, in various forms, Galenists claimed], then women, whose bodies also produced menstrual blood, could conceive on their own, without men" (Thomasset, "The Nature of Woman," 57).

81. See *Hermetica: The Greek Corpus Hermeticum and the Latin Asclepius*, trans. Brian P. Copenhaver (Cambridge, 1992). Marsilio Ficino published a translation of the *Pimander* in 1471, and the French humanist Jacques Lefèvre d'Etaples published a commentary on it in 1494 (*Hermetica*, trans. Copenhaver, xlviii-xlix). The Pimander is parts 1-14 of the *Corpus Hermeticum*. The passage referred to by Agrippa is 12.12: "Notice this also, my child, that to mankind—but not to any other mortal animal—God has granted these two things, mind and reasoned speech, which are worth as much as immortality. [Mankind also has the speech that he utters.] If one uses these gifts as he should, nothing will distinguish him from the immortals; instead, when he has left the body, both these gifts will guide him to the troop of the gods and the blessed" (ibid., 45).

man?[82] Is not woman more fluent, eloquent, and effusive in speech than man? Did we not first learn to speak from our mothers or from our nurses?[83] Without doubt nature itself, architect of the world, in its far-seeing wisdom toward the human race, has accorded this privilege to the female sex, making it difficult to find anywhere a mute woman. It is certainly beautiful and praiseworthy to surpass men at precisely the point at which humans are particularly superior to all other living creatures.

But let us turn from profane texts to those that are our own, i.e., Holy Scripture, and let us in this matter take our point of departure from the sources of religion itself.

We know with certainty that God blessed man because of woman, inasmuch as man had been judged unworthy to receive this blessing before the creation of woman.[84] This is the meaning of the proverb from Solomon: "He who finds a good wife finds happiness, and he receives a blessing from the Lord."[85] And of this passage from Ecclesiasticus: "Happy the husband whose wife is good, the number of their years will be doubled."[86] No man can be compared in dignity to the one who has been worthy of having a good wife.[87] For as Ecclesiasticus says: "A good wife is a grace beyond all grace."[88] This is why Solomon in Proverbs calls her the crown of her husband[89] and Paul the glory of her husband.[90] For the glory, by definition, is the completion and the point of perfection of the being that rests on and is delighted in its end when nothing more can be added to it in order to augment its perfection.

Woman is therefore the completion, perfection, happiness, the blessing

82. See Hesiod, *Theogony*, 75–104; and his *Works and Days*, 101–4 and 763–64.

83. See n. 181, reference to Quintilian.

84. Gen. 1:28. Rodríguez offers this as reason 9 for the superiority of women (220).

85. Prov. 18:22.

86. Ecclus. (Sirach) 26:1. This entire chapter is on women.

87. Agrippa is here following Rodríguez, reason 45, who cites Ecclesiasticus. I find no corresponding passage in Ecclesiasticus; those cited by the Spanish editor of Rodríguez's works do not fit (251 and 251 n. 253b)

88. Ecclus. (Sirach) 26:15: "A modest wife adds charm to charm, and no balance can weigh the values of a chaste soul." The Vulgate 26:19 reads: "A holy and shamefaced woman is grace upon grace." Agrippa's source is probably Rodríguez, who offers this as reason 44 for the superiority of women (251).

89. Prov. 12:4. Rodríguez cites this as reason 46 for the superiority of women (251).

90. 1 Cor. 11:7 This verse, used by misogynists throughout the centuries, is discussed in the introduction. Agrippa—again among many instances—is reverting the tradition by using its own texts against it. Rodríguez says the woman is the glory of man and makes this reason 49 for the superiority of women. He does not, however, cite Paul (252).

and glory of man, and, as Augustine says, the first companion of the human race in this mortal life.[91] This is why every human being necessarily loves her, for the one who will not love her, who hates her, is excluded from every virtue and grace and is even lacking the nature of a human being. Perhaps the mysteries of the Kabbala should be mentioned here, explaining how Abram, having obtained the blessing of God through his wife Sara[h], was called Abraham,[92] the letter H taken from the name of the wife and added to the name of the man, and how also the blessing was acquired for Jacob through a woman, his mother.[93] One finds many similar passages in Holy Scripture, but this is not the place to develop them.

THE SUPERIOR ROLE OF WOMEN IN SALVATION

So then the blessing has been given because of woman, but the law because of man, and this was a law of wrath and curse; for it was to the man that the fruit of the tree had been prohibited,[94] and not to the woman who had not yet been created. God wished her to be free from the beginning; it was therefore the man who committed the sin in eating, not the woman, the man who brought death, not the woman. And all of us have sinned in Adam, not in Eve,[95] and we are infected with original sin not from our mother, who is a

91. Augustine, *De Genesi ad litteram*, 9.3–11 (*PL*, 34:395–400); *The Literal Meaning of Genesis*, 2.73–83. Augustine says the companionship of man and woman resides in procreation and in nothing else. Indeed, in all other respects, for a man the companionship of another man would be preferable. In his later *City of God*, however, he emphasizes mutuality much more, even accepting the possibility of a marriage held together by erotic delight rather than by procreation (12.22, 23, 28; 19.15). Agrippa takes the broadest possible interpretation of Augustine, drawn from the later writings. Thomas Aquinas had adopted the more narrow interpretation—the one Agrippa is opposing—maintaining that procreation is the only way in which woman is a help to man (*Summa Theologica*, I.92.1) See the discussion of these two sides of the question in Turner, *One Flesh*, chap. 3.

92. In Gen. 17:5 Abraham is so called because he is to be "the father of a multitude of nations." In Gen. 17:15, according to the Vulgate, "Sarai" is to be changed to "Sarah." Agrippa changes it from "Sarah" to "Sara," making the point that by giving the letter "h" of her name to Abraham, God's blessing of Abraham passed through the woman.

93. Gen. 27–28.

94. Gen. 2:16–17. Rodríguez cites this as reason 10 for the superiority of women.(220).

95. Rom. 5:12. It was a commonplace among misogynists to argue that Eve was responsible for original sin. Perhaps the most famous passage is Tertullian's in *On the Apparel of Women*: every woman, he says, should walk "about as Eve mourning and repentant, in order that by every garb of penitence she might the more fully expiate that which she derives from Eve—the ignominy, I mean, of the first sin, and the odium (attaching to her as the cause) of human perdition. 'In pains and in anxieties dost thou bear (children), woman; and toward thine husband (is) thy inclination, and he lords it over thee' [Gen. 3:16, English from the Septuagint]. And do you not know

woman, but from our father, a man. Moreover, the ancient law ordained the circumcision of all males[96] but left women uncircumcised, deciding without doubt to punish original sin in the sex that had sinned. And besides, God did not punish the woman for having eaten, but for having given to the man the occasion of evil, which she did through ignorance, tempted as she was by the devil. The man sinned in all knowledge, the woman fell into error through ignorance and because she was deceived.[97] For she was also the first whom the devil tempted, knowing that she was the most excellent of creatures, and, as Bernard says: "The devil, seeing her admirable beauty and knowing that this beauty was the same that he had known in the divine light when he possessed it, that he enjoyed beyond all the other angels in conversation with God, directed his envy against the woman alone, by reason of her excellence."[98]

Christ, born into our world in the greatest humility, took the more humble male sex and not the more elevated and noble female sex, in order to expiate by this humility the arrogant sin of the first father. In addition, because we have been condemned on account of the sin of the man and not of the woman, God wished that this sin be expiated by the sex that had sinned and that atonement come through the same sex that had been deceived in ignorance.[99] This is why God said to the serpent that the woman, or rather, according to a better reading, the seed of the woman, would crush his

---

that you are (each) an Eve? The sentence of God on this sex of yours lives in this age: the guilt must of necessity live too. *You* are the devil's gateway; *you* are the first deserter of the divine law; *you* are she who persuaded him whom the devil was not valiant enough to attack. *You* destroyed so easily God's image, man. On account of *your* desert—that is, death—even the Son of God had to die" (*ANF*, 4:14).

Agrippa repeats the argument he makes here in his *De originale peccato disputabilis opinio* (*Debatable Opinion about Original Sin*). See also n. 132 and related text. But it is already present in Rodríguez, reason 13 (221); and in Martin le Franc, *Le Champion des dames* (Campaux, *La Question des femmes*, 20). Christine de Pizan does not go so far in her *Book of the City of Ladies*, declaring only that if humanity fell through Eve it has been elevated by the Virgin Mary further than it fell (24).

96. Gen. 17:10–14; see also Jer. 4:4.

97. See Gen. 3:13–14. Rodríguez offers this as reason 12 for the superiority of women (221). Isotta Nogarola had argued similarly in a debate with Ludovico Foscarini during the early 1450s in Italy that Eve sinned out of ignorance while Adam was more knowing and therefore more guilty. See King and Rabil, *Her Immaculate Hand*, 57–69.

98. Agrippa's source is Rodríguez, reason 11 (220–21). A check of the index under "Eve" and "diabolus" in *PL* 185 containing the works of Bernard turned up nothing resembling this quotation—if indeed it is a quotation.

99. The argument that Christ was born a man because it was a man who committed the original sin that brought death is reason 26 in Rodríguez (237–38).

head,[100] and not the man or the seed of the man. Perhaps also this explains why the priesthood was conferred by the church on man rather than on woman, because every priest represents Christ, and Christ represents the first person who sinned, that is, Adam himself.[101] One can thus understand the canon that begins with the words "this image" to assert that the woman has not been made in the image of God, that is to say, in corporeal resemblance to Christ.[102]

Moreover, God—I speak of Christ—has not chosen to be the son of a man, but of a woman, whom he has honored to the point that he became incarnate from a woman alone. For Christ is called son of man because of a woman, not because of a husband. This is an extraordinary miracle, which causes the prophet to be astounded, that a woman has encircled a man as a protection, since the male sex has been engulfed by a virgin who carried Christ in her body.[103]

Moreover, when Christ rose from the dead, he appeared first to women, not to men.[104] And it is well known that after the death of Christ some men abjured their faith, although no text attests that women abandoned the faith and the Christian religion.[105] Still further, no persecution, no heresy, no ab-

100. Gen. 3:15.

101. 1 Cor. 15:45.

102. See Gratian, *Decretum*, 2, causa 33, quaestio 5, canon 13. This text, which states that the image of God belongs to the man only, is preceded by a text stating that women ought to be subject to their husbands.

103. *Mulier circumdedit virum:* see Jer. 31:22. The remarkable thing, according to Agrippa's argument, is not that Mary surpassed *her* sex but that she and her sex surpass the male sex. Rodríguez offers this as reason 25 for the superiority of women (237).

   The Virgin Mary is a second Eve and her role is widely viewed as analogous to that of Christ, as Agrippa states here. Such a view of her had been current during the Middle Ages (see text at n. 78) but became very important during the Counter Reformation. She is the image of perfect womanhood but, of course, no more imitable in this than Christ as the son of God is imitable. See Maclean, 23–24 and sources cited; and Ruth Kelso, *Doctrine for the Lady of the Renaissance*, 274–76. See also Marina Warner, *Alone of All Her Sex: The Myth and Cult of the Virgin Mary* (New York, 1983).

104. See Mark 16:1–8 (and parallels in Matt. 28:1–10 and Luke 24:1–11); John 20:1–18. The argument appears in medieval texts and in Rodríguez, reason 32 for the superiority of women (240–41). See the following note.

105. Rodríguez offers as reason 31 for the superiority of women that men lost their faith while Christ was still alive but that no woman did. Rodríguez also says in reason 29 that it was men who crucified Christ (239–40). Agrippa's point is different: that men abjured their faith after Christ's death, while no woman did. Various church fathers make the point that the women's coming to the tomb was an act of faith, even if, as in Mark 16:8, Matt. 28:4–8, and Luke 24:11, they were frightened. In Matthew and Luke they tell the disciples, even though afraid, that they have discovered the empty tomb. In John 20:17 Jesus instructs Mary Magdalene to tell the other disciples that he is risen. See n. 163 and related text.

erration in faith ever occurred because of the deeds of women; one knows that it was otherwise with men.[106] Christ was betrayed, sold, bought, accused, condemned, suffered the passion, was put on a cross, and finally delivered to death only by men.[107] Even more, he was denied by Peter who loved him and abandoned by all the other disciples; only some women accompanied him to the cross and the tomb.[108] Even a pagan, the wife of Pilate, made greater efforts to save Jesus than any of the men who had believed in him.[109] Add to this the fact that theologians almost unanimously agree that the church at that time dwelled only in a single woman, the Virgin Mary, which makes it fitting to call the female sex religious and holy.

If one says with Aristotle that, among all living beings, the males are more courageous, wise, and noble,[110] the apostle Paul, who was a more excellent teacher than he, responds in these words: "God has chosen foolish things of the world to confound the wise, God has chosen the weak of the world to confound the strong; and God has chosen vile things and those that are despised, things which are not, in order to reduce to nothing things which are."[111]

THE POWER OF WOMEN

Who among men stood higher than Adam in all the gifts of the grace of nature? But a woman brought him down. Who was stronger than Samson? A woman overcame his strength. Who was more chaste than Lot? A woman provoked him to incest. Who was more religious than David? A woman troubled his holiness. Who was wiser than Solomon? A woman deceived him.[112]

106. Rodríguez says in reason 33 that men were the first persecutors of Christians and in reason 35 that men are the originators of all heresies (241, 242).

107. Ibid., reason 29.

108. On Peter see Mark 14:66–72 and parallels: Matt. 26:69–75; Luke 22:55–62; John 18:15–18, 25–27. On the women see Mark 15:40–41; Luke 23:27, 49, 55–56.

109. Matt. 27:19.

110. Aristotle, *History of Animals*, 4.11, 538b; 9.1, 608a–b; *Parts of Animals*, 3.1, 661b–662a.

111. 1 Cor. 1:27–28.

112. On Adam and Eve see Gen. 3.

Samson's first wife "brought him down" in Judg. 14—he left her as a result. Delilah did so again in Judg. 16, and that time it cost him his life.

On Lot see Gen. 19:30–38.

2 Kings 11 is the story of the attempt of Athaliah to kill the children of the dead king Ahaziah—a descendant of David—and rule in their stead, an attempt thwarted by Jehosheba, who hid Joash (or Jehoash), the son of Ahaziah, for six years, after which Athaliah was slain and Joash began to rule. In Ps. 89:21–22 God says that he will be with David and that his enemies

Who demonstrated more patience than Job? The devil despoiled him of all his goods, killed his household and children, covered his entire body with ulcers and pus, overwhelming him with pain, and yet could not dislodge him from his original simplicity and patience of spirit and provoke him to anger; yet a woman provoked him, superior to the devil in this respect, and more daring than he, and incited him to use abusive language.[113]

Even Christ himself—if it is allowed to compare him in this way, he who surpasses every other in power and wisdom, since the power and wisdom of God are eternal—does he not allow himself to be tested by a simple woman from Canaan? He said to her: "It is not fair to take the bread of children and throw it to dogs"; she responded to him: "Certainly, Lord, but even the dogs eat the crumbs which fall from the table of their masters"; and when Christ now saw that he was no longer able to prevail over her with this argument, he blessed her and said: "Let it be done as you wish."[114] Who burned with a faith more ardent than Peter, the first of the apostles? A woman led him who was not the least pastor of the church to deny Christ.[115] However much the canonists wish to say that their church cannot err, a woman deceived the church by her extraordinary imposture as pope.[116]

But someone may say that such facts do not add to the glory of women

---

shall not outwit him; 2 Sam. 7:18–29 is a prayer of David petitioning God that his house may last forever; 2 Sam. 11:1–29 is the story of David and Bathsheba.

This last story is the only one that actually fits the text. See 1 Kings 3:1; 11:1–8. Only 11:1–8 speaks of Solomon being deceived because he followed the goddesses (Ashtoreth and Milcom) of his wives. No specific woman is mentioned here.

113. In Job 2:9–10 he refuses to "curse God and die" as his wife enjoined him to do; but in 3:1–3 he did curse the day of his birth. His curse, however, follows upon a visit of three friends; the text is not related to Job's wife.

114. See Matt. 15:21–28. Matthew takes this story from Mark 7:24–30, though in the sixteenth century it was believed that Mark was a summary of Matthew. Christine de Pizan uses this same example in her *Book of the City of Ladies*, 28, to make the same point.

115. See Mark 14:66–72 and parallels in Matt. 26:69–75 and Luke 22:56–60; and John 18:17 (in all of which a woman asks Peter whether he knows Jesus).

116. Agrippa's source is probably Boccaccio, *Concerning Famous Women*, chap. 99. The legend of a female pope first appears in the thirteenth century in the chronicle of the Dominican Jean de Mailly and was repeated by various writers during the following centuries. According to the story, about the year 1100 (later versions say 885), a woman in male disguise, after a distinguished career as a scholar, became pope. Two years later, during a procession to the Lateran, she gave birth to a child and died immediately afterwards. There is no evidence in favor of the story, though it was widely believed in the Middle Ages. It may have been derived from an ancient Roman folk tale. See *The Oxford Dictionary of the Christian Church*, ed. F. L. Cross (London, 1961), 728; see also Alain Boureau, *La papesse Jeanne* (Paris, 1988). The story illustrates the easy association made between learning and lasciviousness in a woman.

but to their censure.[117] Women will respond to that: "If it is necessary that of the two of us one loses goods or even life, I prefer that you lose rather than to be lost myself." In speaking this way they will follow the example of Innocent III, who, in a decretal letter addressed to a certain cardinal sent by the Holy See, left the following message: "If it happens that of the two of us one is to be confounded, I shall choose that you be confounded."[118] Besides, even the civil laws have accorded to women permission to look to their own interests at the expense of someone else.[119]

Does one not see also in Holy Scripture the iniquity of the woman more often blessed and praised than the good actions of the man?[120] Is not Rachel praised, who dreamed up a very clever story to deceive her own father when he sought his idols? And is not Rebecca also praised because she obtained his father's blessing for Jacob by a trick and later more cleverly placated his brother's anger? Rahab the harlot deceived the men who sought the spies of Joshua, and that was reckoned to her as righteousness. Jahel went out to meet Sisera and said to him: "Come to my house, my lord"; and when he asked her for water, she gave him some milk to drink instead and covered him when he lay down; but when Sisera was asleep, she entered secretly, she drove a nail into his head and killed this man who had entrusted himself to her loyalty to be saved. And for this notorious treason, the Scripture says: "Blessed, blessed among women is Jahel in her tent."[121]

117. See John 8:1–11, the story of the woman taken in adultery, which ends with Jesus asking anyone who is without sin to cast the first stone and refusing to judge the woman himself.

118. See Gregory IX, *Decretals*, 1.8, De auctoritate et usu pallii, cap. 3, nisi. The decretal is from Pope Innocent III (1198–1216) and discusses the effects of the concession of the Greek mantle.

119. See *Digest*, 9.2.49, Ad legem Aquiliam. The "Lex Aquilia" annulled all laws previously enacted with reference to the reparation of unlawful damage, whether these were the Twelve Tables or others. The passage is from Ulpian. Ulpian cites Celsus, who stated that in the case of a person who destroyed an adjoining house impelled by a just apprehension that the fire might reach his premises, and whether the fire did so or was previously extinguished, an action under the "Lex Aquilia" cannot be brought. Although the passage does not speak about women, it can be stretched to extend to all who prefer their own self-interest to that of another.

120. Agrippa reverses Scripture (apocrypha) here. Ecclus. 42:14: "Better is the wickedness of a man than a woman who does good; and it is a woman who brings shame and disgrace." After giving examples to support his assertion, Agrippa repeats it at the end of the paragraph. Telle says that in this reversal Agrippa became heretical (*L'Oeuvre de Marguerite d'Angoulême*, 49). Angenot comments that the text from Ecclesiasticus and the counterassertion of Agrippa were both repeated endlessly by subsequent writers (*Les Champions des Femmes*, 23).

121. On Rachel see Gen. 31:19, 31–35. On Rebecca see Gen. 27 and 33. On Rahab see Josh. 2 and 6:22–25; there is an echo here of Rom. 4:22: "his faith was reckoned to him as righteousness." On Jahel and Sisera, see Josh. 4; the story continues in Josh. 5; the citation is from Josh 5:24.

Read the story of Judith and pay attention to what she said to Holofernes: "Listen to the words of your maidservant; for if you follow them, the Lord will make you perfect. I shall come and tell you everything and as a result I shall lead you to the center of Jerusalem, and you will have all the people of Israel as a shepherd has his sheep, and not even a single dog will bark, since these things have been told to me through the providence of God." Then, once Holofernes was lulled to sleep by these flattering words, she struck him in the neck and cut off his head.[122] What more wicked counsel, I implore you, what more cruel trap, what more deceiving treachery could be imagined? And it is for this that the Scripture blesses, praises, and exalts her and that the iniquity of a woman was judged infinitely superior to the good actions of a man.[123]

The clearest possible proof to everyone that can be brought forth for the preeminence of so fortunate a sex is that the noblest of all creatures, the one whom no one ever excelled or ever will excel in dignity, was a woman: I speak of the Blessed Virgin Mary herself, than whom, since she was conceived without original sin, not even Christ is greater so far as his human nature is concerned. Indeed, this argument of Aristotle's is valid: when the best in one species is more noble than the best in another species, the first of

---

122. Jud. 11:4, 15–16 (11:5–19 is Judith's entire speech to Holofernes); 13:6–10.

123. At this point in the text there follows a passage that does not appear in the Antwerp edition published by Agrippa, but only in an edition published at Grenoble probably near the end of the century and preserved at the library of Grenoble. According to the French editors of the critical edition, it is full of errors. The text is doubtless not by Agrippa but by another hand, which is why I place it in a note and not in the main body of the declamation:

> Did not Cain do a good thing in offering for sacrifice the first fruits of his finest crops? But for this good deed he was rejected by God [Gen. 4:3–5]. Was not Esau doing a good act when, in respectful obedience, he went hunting for food for his decrepit father, and he was nonetheless deprived of his blessing and hated by God [Gen. 27:3–4, 30–34]. Uzzah, burning with piety, prevented a leaning Ark from falling over and was struck dead immediately [2 Sam. 6:3–7]. At the moment when king Saul prepared to sacrifice to God the fattest victims of the Amalechites, he was chased from his throne and delivered over to an evil spirit [1 Sam. 15–16]. The daughters of Lot are exonerated of their incest with their father, but their father, despite his drunkenness, is not exonerated, and his descendants are rejected by the church of God [Gen. 19:30–38]. The incestuous Tamar is exonerated and considered more righteous than the patriarch Judah [Gen. 38:11–30], and by her fraudulent incest she earned the right to perpetuate the savior's lineage [Matt. 1:3; Luke 3:33].
>
> Come now you strong and robust men, you scholastic heads pregnant with wisdom, bound with so many bonds, prove by as many examples the opposite thesis, that the iniquity of the man is better than the good actions of the woman. Without doubt, you will not be able to maintain it, without having recourse to allegories, by the use of which the prestige of the woman will equal that of the man. But let us return without delay [to our thesis].

these species is more noble than the second.[124] Among women, the best of her species is the Virgin Mary; among men, no one has surpassed John the Baptist;[125] and there is not a Catholic who does not know how much the Virgin Mary is superior to him, she who was elevated above all the choirs of angels.[126]

One could argue in a similar fashion that when the worst in one species is more evil than the worst in another species, the first species also is inferior to the second. Now we know already that man is the most vicious and the worst of all creatures, whether he was Judas who betrayed Christ and of whom Christ said "It would be better for this man if he had never been born" or an Antichrist worse than him who will one day appear, in whom all the power of Satan will dwell.[127] In addition, Scripture recounts to us that very many men have been condemned to eternal torments, although one reads nowhere that a woman was so condemned.[128]

As additional evidence add a prerogative given to the lower orders of nature: the fact that the queen of all birds and the most noble among them, the eagle, is always found female, never male.[129] The Egyptians have reported on the one hand that there was only one Phoenix and that it was female.[130] On the other hand, the royal serpent, whom they call *basiliskos*, the

124. The statement does indeed sound much like Aristotle and his view of nobility, but several of us who have attempted to do so have been unable to locate the passage.

125. Matt. 11:11.

126. This echoes a view already current in the Middle Ages. See the text at n. 78 and the introduction.

127. The quotation is from Mark 14:21, parallel Matt. 26:24. On the Antichrist, see 1 John 4:3; 2 John 7; Rodríguez offers as reason 36 for the superiority of women that the prophesied Antichrist will be a man (242–43).

128. There are a number of passages in the New Testament that could be intended here, though none of them clearly refers to men as opposed to women; e.g., Matt. 18:8: "And if your hand or your foot causes you to sin, cut it off and throw it away; it is better for you to enter life maimed or lame than with two hands or two feet to be thrown into the eternal fire." See also Matt. 25:46; Luke 16:22–26; 2 Thess. 1:9; Heb. 6:2; Jude 1:6, 7.

129. Varro, *On the Latin Language*, 8.7, mentions the fact that *aquila*, "eagle," denotes both the male and the female. Both Aristotle (*History of Animals*, 9.32, 618b–619a) and Pliny (*Natural History*, 10.3–6) discuss the eagle at length, but neither makes the assertion Agrippa does here.

130. Herodotus, 2.73, discusses the Phoenix in relation to the Egyptians, but he represents the bird as male. Pliny says that according to the story there is only one Phoenix, it lives 540 years, and a new bird arises from its rotting corpse; he does not say anything about the gender of the word "Phoenix" (*Natural History*, 10.2). The Phoenix was known in classical antiquity as a bird resurrected from its own ashes. The origin of the fable is unknown. A poem, attributed to the Christian writer Lactantius (260–330), tells the story. In this poem the bird is female. There is a prose translation in *ANF*, 7:324–26.

most deadly of all venomous serpents, is always male and cannot be born female.[131]

The excellence, goodness, and innocence of women can be amply enough proved by the fact that men, not women, are the origin of all evils. In fact, the first human creature, Adam, because he dared to transgress the law of the Lord, closed the doors of heaven and made us all subject to sin and death.[132] For we have all sinned and we die in Adam, not in Eve.[133] Moreover, his eldest son [Cain] opened the doors of Hell: he was the first envious person, the first homicide, the first fratricide, the first who despaired of the mercy of God. The first bigamist was Lamech. The first to get drunk was Noah; the first to bare the shamefulness of his father was Ham, the son of Noah. The first to be at once tyrant and idolater was Nimrod. The first adulterer was a man; the first incestuous person was a man.[134] In addition, men were the first to make alliance with demons and to discover the human sciences.[135] The

131. Pliny, *Natural History*, 8.33.78 (LCL, 3:57–59), refers to its deadliness to human beings (and to other animals—weasels excepted—and even to bushes) but does not confirm the assertion that it is only male.

132. Agrippa is probably thinking of Rom. 5:12 where Paul says: "Therefore as sin came into the world through one man, and death through sin . . . " (NRSV). Rodríguez says (reason 11) that the woman was tempted first but excused because of her beauty (220–21). In reason 23, devoted to the great crimes committed by men, Rodríguez begins with the assertion Agrippa makes here about Adam (232). In fact, many of the examples offered by Agrippa in the remainder of this paragraph are found in Rodríguez's reason 23, though the two writers are not precisely parallel.

Agrippa says earlier in this text that Adam was responsible for sin and that woman was excused because of her beauty (see n. 95 and text related to nn. 95 and 101). Here the argument is stated in a way much more strongly favorable to women.

133. 1 Cor. 15:21–22.

134. On Cain and Abel see Gen. 4:1–16.

On Lamech see Gen. 4:19; Lamech's two wives were Adah and Zillah. Most of the examples immediately following are found also in Rodríguez, reason 23 (231ff.).

On Noah's drunkenness see Gen. 9:21; on his exposure by Ham see Gen. 9:22.

On Nimrod see Gen. 10:8–9. The text says only that Nimrod was a great hunter; it says nothing of his being a tyrant and idolater.

There is no clear biblical reference to the first case of adultery. The first case of incest mentioned is that of Lot with his daughters, Gen. 19:30–38. The daughters, however, took the initiative in this instance.

135. *Prophanas artes*: "Profane" means that which is not dedicated to religious use, hence secular. I call attention to the expression because further on Agrippa will credit women with the invention of the liberal arts. See below, text related to n. 155, where he makes this statement explicitly, and then nn. 173, 175–77, and 190 and related texts.

sons of Jacob were the first men to sell their brother; the Egyptian Pharaoh first killed his male children. Men were the first to devote themselves to excesses against nature (witness Sodom and Gomorrah, cities at other times celebrated, which the sins of men caused to perish).[136]

We read that men everywhere, by virtue of their rash sensuality, were bigamists, had numerous wives and numerous concubines, and were adulterers and fornicators. There were, for example, numerous spouses and concubines of men such as Lamech, Abraham, Jacob, Esau, Joseph, Moses, Samson, Elkanah, Saul, David, Solomon, Ashhur, Rehoboam, Abijah, Caleb, Ahasuerus,[137] and innumerable others who, in addition to several spouses,

136. On the selling of Joseph see Gen. 37:25–28. On Pharaoh's killing his male children see Exod. 1:16. On Sodom and Gomorrah see Gen. 18:21.

137. Gen. 4:23 mentions two wives of Lamech: Adah and Zillah.

Gen. 16 is the story of Sarah giving her maid Hagar to Abraham as a wife. Gen. 25:1–2 mentions another wife of Abraham, Keturah, who bore him six children. Gen. 25:6 states that Abraham also had concubines.

Gen. 29 is the story of Jacob working seven years for Rachel but then receiving Leah instead and having to work seven more years for Rachel. Gen. 46:15 states that altogether Jacob's sons and daughters numbered thirty-three. He therefore had a number of other wives (and/or concubines) as well, who are not mentioned by name.

Gen. 36:1–5 mentions three wives of Esau from among the Canaanites: Adah, Oholibamah, and Basemath.

In Gen. 41:45 Joseph is given Asenath in marriage by Pharaoh, and she bore him two sons, Manasseh and Ephraim (41:50–52). She is the only wife and they are the only sons of Joseph mentioned. See the end of the Joseph cycle, Gen. 50:23.

Only one wife of Moses is mentioned, Zipporah, daughter of a Midianite priest Jethro (Exod. 3:1; 4:18; 18:1ff.), but also called Hobab (Num. 10:29; Judg. 4:11). Zipporah bore Moses two sons, Gershon (Exod. 2:22; 18:3) and Eliezer (Exod. 18:4). These are the only sons of Moses mentioned.

Judg. 15:1–3 mentions a wife of Samson whose father thought that he hated her, so he gave her to another man. In Judg. 16:1 Samson lies with a harlot and in 16:4 with another (Delilah). See n. 150 and related text.

1 Sam. 1:1–2 mentions two wives of Elkanah: Hannah and Peninnah. It is also said here that Hannah bore no children but Peninnah did. 1 Chron. 6:25–27 mentions eight sons of Elkanah but says nothing about who bore them.

1 Sam. 14:49–50 mentions one wife of Saul, and nowhere else is Saul said to have other wives or mistresses. However, in 2 Sam. 2:8 Ishbosheth, not mentioned in 1 Sam. 14:49–50, is mentioned as a son of Saul; thus Saul had sons by more than one wife.

The first mention of a wife for David is Saul's daughter Merab (1 Sam. 18:17–27). He married Abigail after her husband died (1 Sam. 25:38–42), a passage that goes on to say that David also took Ahinoam of Jezreel as his wife (25:43). A number of other wives and the sons they bore David are listed in 2 Sam. 3:2–5. The story of David and Bathsheba (the mother of Solomon, David's successor) is told in 2 Sam. 12. Ten concubines are mentioned in 2 Sam. 20:3. See also 1 Kings 1:1–4.

1 Kings 11:1–8 alludes to many foreign wives of Solomon and the temples he built for the gods they brought with them from foreign lands.

also had mistresses and concubines. And their union with these women did not suffice to satiate their desire; they also had relations with the maidservants of these women. But we do not find any woman, with the single exception of Bathsheba,[138] who was not always contented with a single husband, and none can be found who remarried when she had a child by her first husband. The reason is that women are much more modest, chaste, and continent than men.[139]

THE SUPERIOR CONSTANCY OF WOMEN ILLUSTRATED

Our readings teach us that when women are found sterile, they often abstain from lying with their husbands, and they bring in to him another woman, for example, Sarah, Rachel, Leah, and many other sterile women, who brought to their husbands their maidservants in order that they might raise up a posterity for their husbands.[140] But, let me ask, was there ever a husband so old, frigid, sterile, and incapable of the conjugal act that he had enough affection and goodwill toward his wife to put in his place another man capable of bedewing her fertile womb with fertile semen? We read, however, that Lycurgus and Solon in ancient times passed laws according to which if an old man, having passed the age of marriage or unfit to love for some other reason, had married a young girl, the latter had the right to choose among his kinsman a young man, notable in vigor and character, to share with her the sweet

---

1 Chron. 4:5–8 mentions two wives of Ashhur and the sons they bore him.

2 Chron. 11:18–21 states that Rehoboam had in all eighteen wives and sixty concubines, who bore him twenty-eight sons and sixty daughters.

2 Chron. 13:21 states that Abijah took fourteen wives and had twenty-two sons and sixteen daughters.

1 Chron. 2:18–19 says that Caleb married Azubah and that when she died he married Ephrath, who bore him a son. But Jerioth, whom he presumably did not marry, bore him three sons as well.

In Esther, Ahasuerus (= Xerxes) is the king of Persia. Esther is one of many beautiful women who are brought to lie with the king after the king rejected his wife Vashti for refusing to come into his presence when commanded. Esther was more pleasing to him than all the others, and he married her.

138. See n. 49.

139. Rodríguez, reason 15, also says women are much more chaste than men, but his discussion does not parallel Agrippa's (224–27).

140. See Gen. 16:2 (Sarah); Gen. 30:3 (Rachel); Gen. 30:9 (Leah). See also Plutarch, *Bravery of Women*, chap. 21, on Stratonice, who, unable to have children of her own, chose a beautiful slave by whom her husband could have children and then brought them up as if they had been her own (LCL, *Moralia*, 3:555–57).

play and frolicking of love, on condition that if she bore an infant it was declared to be her husband's and was not to be called a bastard or illegitimate.[141] We read that these laws were indeed passed, but we do not read that they were observed, not so much because of the hard-heartedness of the men but because of the chastity of the women, which refused them.

There are, in addition, innumerable women, quite illustrious, who, by their signal modesty, have far surpassed men in conjugal love. These include Abigail the wife of Nabal, Artemisia the wife of Mausolus, Argia the wife of the Theban Polynices,[142] Julia the wife of Pompey, Porcia the wife of Cato, Cornelia the wife of Gracchus, Messalina the wife of Sulpicius,[143] Alcestis the wife of Admetus, Hypsicratia the wife of the king of Pontus Mithridates,[144]

---

141. Plutarch, *Life of Lycurgus*, 15.7; *Life of Solon*, 20.2–3.

142. On Abigail, see 1 Sam. 25:1–38.

Cicero writes: "The famous Artemisia, wife of Mausolus, King of Caria, who built the celebrated burial monument at Halicarnassus, lived in sorrow all her days and wasted away under its enfeebling influence" (*Tusculan Disputations*, 3.75 [LCL, 315]). See also Aulus Gellius, 10.18. What is said of her here and later (see below, text related to n. 199) is related in Boccaccio's account in *Concerning Famous Women*, chap. 55, which is doubtless Agrippa's immediate source. Christine de Pizan adapts this story in her *Book of the City of Ladies*, 55–57.

Statius recounts in the *Thebaid* (12:296ff.) the sadness of Argia, daughter of King Adrastus and wife of Polynices, while she seeks the remains of her husband Polynices, to whom (together with Antigone) she renders funeral honors. Boccaccio tells the story in *Concerning Famous Women*, chap. 27. She is also celebrated by Dante in *Purgatory*, 22.110.

143. Julia married Pompey in 59 BCE. In 55 the sight of him returning from the Roman assembly spattered with blood (from having performed a sacrifice) caused her to have a miscarriage. In 54 she died in childbirth. She was buried in the Campus Martius, and in 46 her father, Julius Caesar, held magnificent shows over her tomb. Agrippa's immediate source was probably Boccaccio, *Concerning Famous Women*, chap. 79.

Porcia was not the wife but the daughter of Cato, and the wife of Brutus; Marcia was Cato's wife. Both, however, are examples of conjugal love. On Marcia see Plutarch, *Cato Minor*, 25ff.; Lucan, *Pharsalia*, 2.325–91. On Porcia see Plutarch, *Brutus*, 53; Valerius Maximus, 6.5. Agrippa's immediate source was probably Boccaccio, *Concerning Famous Women*, chap. 80.

Cornelia was the second daughter of Scipio Africanus (who defeated Hannibal). She married Tiberius Sempronius Gracchus and had twelve children by him. After his death in 154 BCE she did not remarry, refusing the hand of Ptolemy VII (Euergetes II), devoting herself to the education in Greek culture of her three surviving children (Tiberius, Gaius, and Sempronia). Tradition made her a model of Roman motherhood. See Plutarch, *Life of Tiberius Gracchus*, 1; Valerius Maximus, 6.1. See also Cicero, *On Divination*, 1.18.36; 2.29.62; Pliny, *Natural History*, 7.36.

The Messalina intended here appears to be the wife of the emperor Claudius who married her paramour Sulpicius in secret (Agrippa cites her as a whore in *Of the Vanitie and Uncertaintie of Artes and Sciences*, 205, where his source was doubtless Juvenal, *Satires*, 6.114–32). She does not represent the conjugal fidelity Agrippa is praising, which makes the reference puzzling. There is no other connection between Sulpicius and Messalina known to me in classical antiquity.

144. Admetus won Alcestis by driving wild beasts yoked to a chariot (with divine assistance). At the bridal feast Admetus forgot to sacrifice to Artemis and on opening the bridal chamber found

and also Dido who founded Carthage, the Roman Lucretia, and Sulpicia the wife of Lentulus.[145]

There are an infinite number of others whose pledge of virginity and modesty could not be altered even by death. The following offer themselves as examples: the Caledonian Atalanta, the Volscian Camilla;[146] the Greeks Iphigenia, Cassandra, and Chryseis.[147] Let us cite further the young Lac-

---

it full of serpents—an omen of imminent death. Apollo persuaded the Fates (having gotten them drunk: Aeschylus, *Eumenides*, 728) to decree that if anyone would die in place of Admetus he could live. Alcestis was the only volunteer. The story is told in Euripides, *Alcestis*. Euripides was the first writer to raise the question of the baseness of Admetus in accepting such an offer. The author of the pseudo-Aristotelian *Economics*, book 3 (3.1)—a text widely cited by Renaissance moralists and regarded by them as by Aristotle—asserts that her fame would never have been so great apart from the adversity of her husband.

Hypsicratia, according to Plutarch, was Mithridates's concubine, not his wife. According to Plutarch's account, she lived in camp with him and fought as a soldier; when Mithridates was about to be defeated by Pompey, he was deserted by all but three followers, of whom she was one. See Plutarch, *Life of Pompey*, 32; Valerius Maximus, 4.6.Ext.2. Agrippa's immediate source was probably Boccaccio, *Concerning Famous Women*, chap. 76.

145. The reference here is to Dido's faithfulness to her husband Sychaeus, who was murdered by Dido's brother Pygmalion. See Virgil, *Aeneid*, 1.343–71. Boccaccio tells this story at the beginning of his account of her life in *Concerning Famous Women*, chap. 40.

Lucretia was raped by Sextus Tarquinius and, after informing her father and her husband—getting from them a pledge to revenge the act—she killed herself. The result was the overthrow of the Tarquin dynasty and the end of kingship in Rome. See Livy, 1.58–60. Boccaccio also recounts the story in his *Concerning Famous Women*, chap. 46. On the Lucretia legend and its revival in fifteenth-century Florence, see *Knowledge, Goodness, and Power: The Debate over Nobility among Quattrocento Italian Humanists*, ed. Albert Rabil, Jr. (Binghamton, N.Y., 1991), 28–29. For a recent controversial discussion of the Lucretia legend, see Stephanie H. Jed, *Chaste Thinking: The Rape of Lucretia and the Birth of Humanism* (Bloomington, Ind., 1989); and the review by Ronald G. Witt in *Renaissance Quarterly*, 43 (1990): 604–6.

Sulpicia followed her husband Lentulus, who had been proscribed by the triumvirate, into Sicily. See Valerius Maximus, 6.7.3. Agrippa's immediate source was probably Boccaccio, *Concerning Famous Women*, chap. 83.

146. See Ovid, *Metamorphoses*, 10.559–704, for the story of Atalanta. Although a virgin goddess, her love was won by Hippomenes, who beat her in a footrace, with the help of Aphrodite, who gave him three golden apples. Because he possessed her on sacred ground before the proper sacrifices had been made, the two were turned into lions. The story (and its variants) does not illustrate Agrippa's point here.

Camilla was dedicated to the goddess Artemis (Diana) by her father; she fought on the side of the Latins against Aeneas and was killed. Her dead body was protected by her patron goddess. See Virgil, *Aeneid*, 11.535–600. Boccaccio tells her story, *Concerning Famous Women*, chap. 37.

147. Iphigenia was the daughter of Agamemnon, leader of the Greeks in the Trojan war. He sacrificed her to obtain favorable winds so his ships could sail for Troy. See Euripides, *Iphigenia at Tauris*, lines 5–41. See also Aeschylus, *Libation Bearers*, 900ff.; Sophocles, *Electra*, 558ff.; Euripides, *Electra*, 1010ff.

Cassandra was the daughter of Priam, king of Troy. In Homer's *Iliad*, 13.365, she is men-

edemonian, Spartan, Milesian, and Theban virgins and innumerable others mentioned in the stories of the Hebrews, Greeks, and Barbarians, who have placed greater value on their virginity than on kingdoms and even their lives.

If one seeks also for examples of filial piety, among others are offered to us the piety of the vestal Claudia toward her father and that of the young plebeian, of whom we have spoken above, toward her mother.[148]

But some Zoilus[149] will throw up as counterexamples to these the baneful marriages of Samson, Jason, Deiphobus, Agamemnon,[150] and similar tragedies. But if anyone examines these situations with the eyes of a lynx (as they say), he will discover that the wives are accused falsely, for no one of them who had a good husband conducted herself in an evil way. In reality it is only evil husbands who have evil wives; the wives were good and were corrupted by the defects of their husbands.[151] If it had been permitted to women

---

tioned as the most beautiful of Priam's daughters, but nothing is said in that book about her prophetic powers. She is best known in mythology as a prophetess doomed to be ignored by everyone. She so appears in Aeschylus, *Agamemnon*, where she dies with Agamemnon. In Virgil's *Aeneid* (2.246) it is she who vainly warns the Trojans against the wooden horse. Boccaccio tells her story in *Concerning Famous Women*, chap. 33.

Chryseis was the daughter of a priest of Apollo, Chryses. She was taken prisoner and given to Agamemnon (Homer, *Iliad*, 1). Her father sought to buy her back from Agamemnon, who refused until Apollo sent a plague on the Greek camp. Agamemnon then relented but compensated himself by taking Briseis from Achilles, thus initiating the quarrel that forms the basic plot of the *Iliad*. Her example does not fit here, for as a prize of war she surely was not virginal, nor could she have vowed virginity.

148. Claudia was a vestal virgin wrongly accused of having violated her vow of chastity. She was justified by a prodigy recounted by Ovid, *Fasti*, 4.305–44. See Boccaccio, *Concerning Famous Women*, chap. 60.

On the plebeian woman, see above, n. 69 and related text.

149. Zoilus of Amphipolis (fourth cent. BCE) was a Cynic philosopher notorious for his bitter attacks on Homer, Plato, and Isocrates. Only fragments of his works survive.

150. In Judg. 15 Samson returns to his wife only to find that his father-in-law, thinking Samson hated her, has betrothed her to another man. See above, n. 137 and related text.

Jason was the leader of the Argonauts who captured the Golden Fleece with the help of Medea, whom he married. The two later became estranged, and in revenge Medea murdered their three children. See Apollonius of Rhodes, *Argonautica*, bk. 3; Euripides, *Medea*. Boccaccio tells this story in *Concerning Famous Women*, chap. 16.

Deiphobus was a son of Priam. In both Homer's *Iliad* (13.155–68) and *Odyssey* (8.517–20) he played a significant role in the Trojan War. Later sources say he was married to Helen after the Trojan War. Helen, seeking to reconcile herself to Menelaus, allowed Menelaus into their bedroom, where Menelaus mutilated and killed him. See Virgil, *Aeneid*, 6.495–534.

Agamemnon was murdered by his wife Clytemnestra upon his return from the Trojan War. See Aeschylus, *Agamemnon*.

151. Rodríguez in reason 21 makes this same point (231), but he does not emphasize it the way Agrippa does. Agrippa repeats it in *Of the Vanitie and Uncertaintie of Artes and Sciences*, chap. 67 (232):

to make laws and to write historical accounts, imagine the number of tragedies they would have been able to write about the enormous wickedness of
men, among whom one finds a multitude of homicides, thieves, rapists,
forgers, arsonists, and traitors. Even in the time of Joshua and of King David
men engaged in plunder, operating in gangs so numerous that they set up
"princes" of their bands;[152] even today there is an infinite number of them.[153]
Hence, all the prisons are filled with men and all gallows everywhere are
laden with the corpses of men.[154]

Women, to the contrary, have invented all the liberal arts,[155] every virtue and benefit, which the very names of the arts and virtues—being feminine in gender—show better than anything. Another remarkable fact is that
even the terrestrial globe itself is called by women's names, the nymph Asia,
Agenor's daughter Europa, Epaphys's daughter Libya, also called Africa.[156]
Finally, a run through all the types of virtues will find a woman holding first
place in every one.

It was in fact a woman, the Virgin Mary herself, who first vowed her
virginity to God and for that merited being the mother of God. Women
prophets have always been inspired by a more divine spirit than men, as is
known about the sibyls from the accounts of Lactantius, Eusebius, and Augustine. Miriam, the sister of Moses, was a prophetess. Likewise, when Jeremiah was in captivity, the wife of his uncle, named Huldah, was elevated—
in preference to a man—to the role of prophetess for the people of Israel
who were going to perish.[157]

"all these incommodities happen not so much through the fault of wives, as through the error of
husbands, for an unhonest wife is not wont to chance to none, but naughty husbands" (spelling
modernized). See also his *Commendation of Matrimony*: "For an evil wife never happeneth but to an
evil husband" (n.p.; spelling modernized).

152. In Josh. 7:2–5 there is a reference to spies and a small army sent to fight but no mention of
independent leaders; 2 Sam. 4:2–3 refers to captains of raiding bands.

153. This is an interesting bit of social commentary. It would be informative to know more
precisely what Agrippa is referring to here.

154. Rodríguez in reason 21 asserts that women are more just than men, that public places are
filled with executed men but no women (230–31).

155. *Omnium artium liberalium*: "All the liberal arts." A "liberal art" is one worthy of a free person.
The phrase is both classical and characteristic of humanist literature.

156. Rodríguez makes the same point, reason 43 (246).

157. For Lactantius see *Divine Institutes*, 1.6 (*ANF*, 7:15–16); Eusebius of Caesarea, *Praeparatio
Evangelica*, 9.15 and 10.11 (*PG*, 21:703–4, 818–27)—Sibylline oracles are mentioned in the first
reference, other oracles in both; Augustine, *City of God*, 3.18; 10.27 (Cumaean Sibyl); 18.24.
    Miriam is mentioned in Exod. 15:20–21 as the sister of Aaron, but Aaron was Moses' brother
(see Exod. 6:20).

Let us read with care the Holy Scriptures and we shall see that the constancy of women in loyalty and the other virtues is extolled far more than that of men; thus Judith, Ruth, and Esther were celebrated with so much glory that they gave their names to books of the Bible. The renowned Abraham, whom Scripture calls righteous because of his faith, since he believed in God, was nonetheless subordinated to his wife Sarah and received from the voice of God the following order: "Whatever Sarah says to you, follow her words in all things."[158] Likewise, Rebecca, firm in her faith, did not hesitate to question God and was judged worthy of obtaining a response from him. She heard the prophecy: "Two nations are from your womb, and two people will be divided from there." The widow of Zarephath believed in Elijah, though he said a hard thing to her.[159]

Likewise Zechariah, convicted of incredulity by the angel, became mute, while his wife Elizabeth prophesied through the infant that she carried in her, and through her words, and received praise for having faithfully believed. She herself then praised the Blessed Virgin Mary in these words: "Happy are you for having believed what has been said to you by the Lord."[160] Likewise, the prophetess Anna, after the revelation of Simeon, confessed her God and spoke of him to everyone willing to listen—those who awaited the deliverance of Israel. Philip had four virgin daughters who prophesied.[161]

What should we say of the Samaritan woman with whom Christ spoke at a well? Filled by the faith of this believing woman, he refused the apostles' food. There is also the faith of the Canaanite woman and of the woman who suffered from a hemorrhage. Did Martha not confess her faith as did Peter?[162] We know also, through the Gospels, the constancy of Mary Mag-

---

In 2 Kings 22:14ff. and 2 Chron. 34:22ff., Huldah is the wife of Shallum. Shallum is also the name of Jeremiah's uncle (Jer. 32:7). It is not at all clear that the two Shallums are the same.

158. On Abraham, whose faith was righteousness, see Gen. 15:6; Rom. 4:3; Galatians 3:6. The quotation is from Gen. 21:12.

159. For the quotation regarding Rebecca see Gen. 25:23. On the widow of Zarephath see 1 Kings 17:8–16; Elijah told her to feed him the little food she had before she fed herself and her son, but he also promised her that she would not run out of meal and oil until God sent rain, a prophecy that was fulfilled. Cf. Luke 4:26.

160. On Zechariah's muteness see Luke 1:20. The quotation is from Luke 1:45.

161. On the prophetess Anna see Luke 2:36–38. On the daughters of Philip see Acts 21:9 and below, nn. 170 and 182 and related texts.

162. On the Samaritan woman see John 4:5–42. On Martha's confession of faith, see John 11:24–27. On the faith of the Canaanite woman see Mark 7:24–30 and the parallel in Matt. 15:21–28. On the woman suffering from a hemorrhage see Mark 5:25–34 and parallels in Matt.

dalene in her faith. For while the priests and the Jews crucify Christ, she cries, carries unguents to the cross, looks for Christ in the tomb, interrogates a gardener, recognizes God. She hastens to tell the apostles and announces to them that Christ is risen. But they doubt while she believes.[163] Again, what about Priscilla? That very holy woman instructed Apollos, bishop of Corinth, one of the apostles, very learned in the law; and this apostle was not ashamed to learn from a woman what he taught in the church.[164]

Let us add that there are not fewer women than men who, in suffering martyrdom and in despising death, have witnessed to the constancy of their faith. And I ought not to pass over here in silence that admirable mother, worthy of being remembered by all people of goodwill, who not only courageously suffered the sight of seven of her sons perishing in cruel martyrdom but bravely exhorted them to accept death and who, herself, confident in God through all her tribulations, died following her sons in order to honor the law of her fathers.[165] And did not Theodelinda, daughter of the king of Bavaria, convert the Lombards; and Greisilla, sister of the emperor Henry I, the Hungarians; Clotilda, daughter of the king of Burgundy, the French; and a woman of humble origin called Apostola the Spanish?[166] Did not each of

---

9:20–22 and Luke 8:43–48. On Martha's confession see John 11:24–27; and on Peter's, see Mark 8:29 and parallels in Matt. 16:16 and Luke 9:20–21; see also John 6:68–69.

163. Rodríguez offers this briefly as reason 27 for the superiority of women (238–39), but he does not elaborate as Agrippa does. In Mark 16:1 Mary Magdalene is mentioned as one of the women who discovered the empty tomb. Parallels to this passage are found in Matt. 27:55–28:10, Luke 23:55–24:12, and John 19:25, 20:1–18. In Mark 16:9–11 she is the first to whom Jesus appears; she goes to tell the disciples but they do not believe her. She is mentioned in Luke 8:2 as the woman from whom Jesus cast out seven demons.

164. Acts 18:2, 24–28.

165. On the mother witnessing the deaths of her seven sons, see 2 Macc. 7. The story is also the principal subject of 4 Macc.. Rodríguez mentions this in passing in reason 23 for the superiority of women (236).

166. Theodelinda, a Catholic princess and daughter of the duke of Bavaria, was married to Authari, king of the Lombards, helping to legitimize his kingship. When he died in 590 his elected successor, Agilulf (591–616), married Theodelinda. The marriage of her daughter Gundeberga to Rothari, duke of Brescia, reestablished Catholicism (as opposed to Arianism—the view that Christ was created by God and so was subordinate and not eternal with the Father) in his kingdom. She died in 625. See C. W. Previté-Orton, *The Shorter Cambridge Medieval History*, 2 vols. (Cambridge, 1960), 1:218, 220.

Greisilla was sister of Henry (876–936), duke of Saxony. Henry's election as king of the Saxons and Thuringians in 919 began the revival of the German monarchy. He initiated the eastward thrust, continued by his son Otto or Otho I (936–73), in whose reign the Slavs were converted to Christianity. Although the Slavs were indeed converted at this time, I find nothing of the role Greisilla might have played analogous to that of Clotilda in the conversion of the

them convert innumerable people to faith in Christ? Finally, this very pious sex alone is preeminently the one in which, up to the present day, the Catholic faith and unending works of devotion shine forth.

THE CONTRIBUTIONS OF WOMEN OF ANTIQUITY
TO THEOLOGY AND PHILOSOPHY, ARTS
AND SCIENCES, AND POLITICS

But in order that no one doubt that women can do everything men do, let us show it by examples; we shall discover that there has never been any exceptional or virtuous deed of any kind performed by men that has not been executed by women with equal brilliance.

In the priesthood of the pagans in earlier times Melissa, priestess of Cybele, stands out; in later times all the other priestesses of this goddess were called Melissas. Likewise, Hypecaustria was the priestess of Minerva; Mera of Venus; Iphigenia of Diana; and the priestesses of Bacchus were celebrated under diverse names: Thyiades, Maenads, Bacchae, Eliades, Mimallonides, Aedonides, Euthyades, Bassarides, Triaterides.[167] Among the Jews Miriam,

---

Franks (see the following paragraph). In a number of sources there is also mentioned Gisela of Bavaria (985–ca. 1065), sister of Duke Henry II of Bavaria, who married Stephen of Hungary in 996. Her cousin, Otto III, made the couple king and queen of Hungary. She exerted a strong Germanic influence on the court and was very pious, giving much of her wealth to the church. See *An Annotated Index of Medieval Women*, ed. Anne Echols and Marty Williams (Oxford, 1992), 201 and sources cited. The modern editor of the 1540 German translation of Agrippa believes this second Gisela is the one intended: Jungmayr, 352 n. 187.

Clotilda is St. Clotilda, a Catholic princess who, in 493, married Clovis, king of the Franks (481–511). Under her influence Clovis and 3,000 other Franks were baptized at Christmas in 496. See Previté-Orton, *Shorter Cambridge Medieval History*, 1:151, 153. Christine de Pizan uses this example in her *Book of the City of Ladies*, 151.

Apostola probably refers to Etheria (late fourth century)—Apostola being incorrectly regarded by Agrippa as a name. She was born on the west seaside of Galicia (the part of Spain that overhangs Portugal and the state in which Rodríguez del Padron also was born), a poor section of the country—which supports the assertion in the text that she was of humble origin. She was famous for traveling to the Holy Land and for an account of her travels, *Eteria: Itinerario*, ed. Juan Monteverdi (Buenos Aires, 1955). There are several twentieth-century biographies of her. See *Oxford Dictionary of the Christian Church*, 466, and *Gran encyclopedia Gallega*, ed. Silverio Cañada (Santiago, Spain, 1980), 11:26–28. I am indebted to the staff of the Hispanic Society of America, New York, for helping me to identify her.

167. Melissa was the daughter of Melissus, king of Crete. According to Lactantius, Melissus appointed his daughter as the first priestess of Cybele, and all subsequent priestesses were named after her. See Lactantius, *Divine Institutes*, 1.22 (*ANF*, 7:37–39). Hypecaustria (Greek Hypekkaustria) is not a name but the title of a priestess of Athena ("one who kindles the fire") in the

together with Moses, entered into the sanctuary with Aaron and was considered a priestess.[168] In our religion, although women are prohibited from exercising the priestly office, we know from published accounts that once a woman who had not revealed her sex succeeded to the sovereign pontificate.[169] Notable also among our coreligionists are the many holy abbesses and nuns whom the ancients did not think unworthy of the name priestess.

In prophecy, among the peoples of the whole world, Cassandra, the Sibyls, Miriam sister of Moses, Deborah, Huldah, Anna, Elizabeth, the four daughters of Philip,[170] and, more recently, many other holy women, such as Bridget and Hildegard,[171] were illustrious.

In magic, an impenetrable science of good and evil spirits, Circe and Medea, above all others, accomplished things far more marvelous than

---

city of Soli in Sicily. See Plutarch, *Moralia: The Greek Questions*, 292.3. Mera, priestess of Venus, is cited by Statius, *Thebaid*, 8.478. The Roman goddess Diana is identified with the Greek goddess Artemis. The temple of Artemis at Corinth was named Iphigenia. See Pausanias, 2.35.1.

Although the French editors of the critical edition suggest that the enumeration of the various names of the priestesses of Bacchus could have been taken from a compiler such as Coelius Rhodiginus (Ludovico Celio Rodrigino, 1453–1525), *Antiquae lectiones*, 16.2, this text was published only in 1599. The names were more likely present in some occult text available to Agrippa, where the variety of names may have had some special significance. The usual names in classical literature for the followers of Bacchus (Dionysius) are the Maenads and the Bacchae.

168. Exod. 15:20. See n. 157 and related text.

169. This is the second reference to the legend of Pope Joan. See n. 116 and related text.

170. See the following notes and related texts. On Cassandra, n. 147; on the Sibyls, n. 157; on Miriam, nn. 157, 168; on Huldah, n. 157; on Anna, n. 161; on Elizabeth, Luke 1:5–80 and n. 160; on the four daughters of Philip, nn. 161, 182. Only Deborah in this list has not been mentioned earlier. On her, see Judg. 4–5, and below, n. 184 and related text. Rodríguez, reason 28, mentions the sibyls and some of the biblical prophecies (239).

171. St. Bridget of Sweden (1303–73) was the daughter of one of the wealthiest landowners of Sweden. She married and had eight children, among whom was St. Catherine of Sweden (1331–81). When her husband died in 1343 she was freed from worldly ties and in 1346 founded the Order of Brigittines, obtaining confirmation for her order from the pope when she went to Rome in 1349. She remained in Rome until her death and aided St. Catherine of Siena (1347–80) in urging the return of Pope Gregory XI from Avignon to Rome. Her visions were held in great repute; she was canonized in 1391.

St. Hildegard of Bingen (1098–1179) was also born of a noble family and was subject to visions from early childhood. She was raised by a recluse and in 1116 joined a Benedictine community, becoming its abbess in 1136. She began to record her visions and received papal approval of them in 1147 (with the help of St. Bernard of Clairvaux). She moved her community to Rupertsberg between 1147 and 1152 and from there founded daughter houses in other locations. She exercised a wide influence on many famous contemporaries. On both Bridget and Hildegard, see *The Oxford Dictionary of the Christian Church*, 198 and 639 and sources cited.

even Zoroaster himself, although he is regarded by many as the inventor of this art.[172]

In addition in philosophy there were the famous Theano, the wife of Pythagoras, and their daughter Dama, renowned in explaining her father's veiled opinions. Celebrated also were Aspasia and Diotima, disciples of Socrates, [Lastheneia of] Mantinea and Axiothea of Phlius, both disciples of Plato. Plotinus exalts Gemina and Amphiclea.[173] Lactantius praises Themista. The Christian church is proud of St. Catherine, a young girl who far surpassed the philosophers of her time in learning. And let us take care not to forget here Queen Zenobia, disciple of the philosopher Longinus, who, because of the breadth and brilliance of her learning, received the name Ephinissa and whose holy works Nicomachus translated into Greek.[174]

172. Circe was very powerful in magic. See Homer, *Odyssey*, 10.210ff.; Virgil, *Aeneid*, 7.19–20. See also Boccaccio, *Concerning Famous Women*, chap. 36.

Medea is "the cunning one," niece of Circe. She was universally regarded as a witch but has a tendency to pass into a goddess. See Apollonius of Rhodes, *Argonautica*, bks. 3–4; Euripides, *Medea*; Ovid, *Metamorphoses*, 7.162ff. See also Boccaccio, *Concerning Famous Women*, chap. 16.

Zoroaster, or Zarathustra (628–551 BCE), was believed to be the author of many works dealing with theology, astrology, and magic. There are many references to him in classical Greek and Hellenistic writers. In his *On Occult Philosophy*, 1.41, Agrippa cites Homer's *Odyssey*, Virgil, Lucan, and Apuleius to illustrate the transformative power of sorcerers. He also cites an anecdote from St. Augustine (worthy of respect because it is from him) in which he says that there are in Italy some sorcerers who transform men into beasts of burden (by giving them cheese) to carry their loads and who turn them back into human form once the work is done.

173. On Theano, daughter of Pythagoras, see Diogenes Laertius, 8:42.

Aspasia was the mistress of Pericles, who divorced his wife to live with her. Socrates claims her as his teacher in rhetoric and says that he believes she wrote the famous oration of Pericles (*Menexenus*, 236ff.). Aristophanes parodies the couple in *Acharnians*, 515–39. The Socratic Aeschines, for one, attests to her intellectual prowess. See Plutarch, *Life of Pericles*, 24.1–7.

Diotima was a priestess at Mantinea and teacher of Socrates. Plato, in *Symposium* 201F–212A, has her deliver an encomium of love.

Lastheneia and Axiothea wore men's clothing. See Diogenes Laertius, 3.46, 4.2. The latter passage reads: "It is said that among those who attended his [Speusippus's] lectures were the two women who had been pupils of Plato, Lastheneia of Mantinea and Axiothea of Phlius" (LCL, 1:375).

Porphyry, in his *Life of Plotinus*, 9, writes: "Several women were greatly attached to him, amongst them Gemina, in whose house he lived, and her daughter, called Gemina, too, after the mother, and Amphiclea, the wife of Ariston, son of Iamblichus; all three devoted themselves assiduously to philosophy" (quoted in Plotinus, *The Enneads*, trans. Stephen MacKenna, 2d ed. revised by B. S. Page [London, 1956], 7).

174. In his *Divine Institutes*, 3.25, Lactantius writes: "Lastly, they never taught any women to study philosophy, except Themiste only, within the whole memory of man" (ANF, 7:95). Themista was the wife of Leontion, a disciple of Epicurus; Epicurus wrote to both Leontion and Themista. See Diogenes Laertius, 10.5.

There were a number of St. Catherines. The one intended here is probably St. Catherine of Alexandria (fourth cent.), who, according to legend, was of exceptional learning. She is, in fact,

Let us turn to oratory and poetry. Here we may cite Armesia, surnamed Androgynea, Hortensia, Lucretia, Valeria,[175] Copiola, Sappho, Corinna, the Roman Cornificia, Erinna of Telos or of Lesbos, who was surnamed the epigrammatist.[176] In Sallust Sempronia and in the legal writers Calpurnia are

---

the patroness of (among others) scholars. On her see *Oxford Dictionary of the Christian Church,* 249 and sources cited.

Boccaccio, *Concerning Famous Women,* chap. 98, mentions Ephinissa learning Greek under the philosopher Longinus and her making summaries of histories in Latin, Greek, and barbarian languages. But he does not mention Nicomachus translating the works of Ephinissa into Greek.

175. Armesia Sentinas pleaded her cause before the praetor L. Titius so eloquently that she won her cause and in doing so seemed so much like a man that she was called Androgynea. See Valerius Maximus, 8.3.1.

Hortensia was the daughter of the famous Roman orator Hortensius who spoke against the heavy taxes imposed on women because of the needs of the state and succeeded by her eloquence in getting the Triumvirs to rescind most of them (Valerius Maximus, 8.3.3). See also Boccaccio, *Concerning Famous Women,* chap. 82.

On Lucretia, whom the French editors surmise is intended here, see n. 145. The German translation of Agrippa has, instead, Luceia (Lucceia), identified as a mime singer in the late republic (Jungmayr, 354 n. 200). This identification fits the context better.

There are several persons named Valeria, none of whom seems to have had anything to do with contributions to oratory or poetry. The most obvious candidate is the daughter of Publicola, because her story follows that of Lucretia (whose name Valeria's follows in Agrippa's text) in chap. 14 of Plutarch's *Bravery of Women* (LCL, *Moralia,* 3:513–17). This Valeria had been sent as a hostage to Tarquin along with other maidens. They all escaped by swimming across the river, whence they had gone, presumably to bathe. The real heroine of this story appears to be Cloelia, who led the others (Cloelia and Valeria are the only two mentioned by name). Porsenna, the Etruscan leader who had sent the women as hostages, admired their bravery. An equestrian statue of a woman was built beside the Sacred Way; some say it was of Cloelia, others that it was of Valeria. Another candidate is a sister of Hortensius the orator (whose daughter, Hortensia, is mentioned here in Agrippa's text), a beautiful woman who enticed Sulla to marry her. She is described as a person of great beauty and splendid birth, but her talent in the story has to do with enticing Sulla to marry her, not with poetry or oratory; she gave birth to Sulla's daughter, Postuma, after his death (Plutarch, *Sulla,* 35.4–5, 37.4; LCL, *Lives,* 4:437–39, 443).

176. Copiola was a player of mimes in Rome. See Pliny, *Natural History,* 7.48.49.

Sappho, the poet from Lesbos, is one of the most famous historical women of antiquity. Boccaccio tells her story: *Concerning Famous Women,* chap. 45. A number of her poems and fragments of poems are extant. See *The Poems of Sappho,* trans. Susy Q. Groden (Indianapolis, 1966).

Corinna was an elder contemporary of the lyrical poet Pindar (518–438 BCE); she wrote narrative lyrical poems on Boeotian subjects for a circle of women. Pausanias writes of her: "Corinna, the only lyric poetess of Tanagra, has her tomb in a conspicuous part of the city, and in the gymnasium is a painting of Corinna binding her head with a fillet for the victory she won over Pindar at Thebes with a lyric poem. I believe that her victory was partly due to the dialect she used, for she composed, not in Doric speech like Pindar, but in one Aeolians would understand, and partly to her being, if one may judge from the likeness, the most beautiful woman of her time" (9.22.3; LCL, 4:265–67). In the *Greek Anthology* she is mentioned by Antipater of Thessalonica, together with Sappho, Erinna, and other female poets (9.26).

Cornificia was the younger sister of Cornificius (d. 42/41 BCE), a famous poet in his time. She

made known.[177] If, in our time, education had not been prohibited to women, today also very well-educated women would be considered more talented than men.[178]

And what do we say of the fact that women seem simply by their very nature and without difficulty to surpass the specialists in all disciplines?

Do not the grammarians pride themselves on being the masters of eloquence? But do we not learn this eloquence much better from our nurses and mothers than from grammarians? Was it not their mother Cornelia who fashioned the remarkable eloquence of the Gracchi?[179] Was it not his Istrian mother who taught Greek to Siles, son of the Scythian king Aripithes?[180] Do not infants born in colonies established in foreign lands always preserve their

---

lived into the Augustan age (beginning 27 BCE) and composed epigrams through which she also achieved renown as a poet equal to that of her brother. See Boccaccio, *Concerning Famous Women*, chap. 84.

Some of Erinna's poems are extant. See the *Greek Anthology*, 6.352; 7.710, 712. For poems on her, see ibid., 7.11–12, 713; 9.190.

177. Sempronia was the mother of Brutus, one of Caesar's assassins. Although Sallust represents her as learned, his emphasis is on her dissoluteness, to which he suggests her learning contributed (Sallust, *The Conspiracy of Catiline*, 25). Boccaccio repeats and even embellishes this picture in *Concerning Famous Women*, chap. 77. These accounts are good examples among many that connected learning in women with dissoluteness. Agrippa here emphasizes only her learning, as also does Christine de Pizan, *Book of the City of Ladies*, 86.

Afrania pleaded her own case in a court of law (Valerius Maximus, 8.3.C), giving rise to an edict prohibiting women from doing so (Ulpian VI ad edict. in *Digest*, III.I.1, par. 5), although the edict only prohibits women from speaking in behalf of others, not from speaking in behalf of themselves. The edict reads:

> Under the second section of the Edict those are referred to who cannot appear for others, and in this portion of it the praetor includes such as are incapacitated by their sex. . . .
>
> On the ground of sex, he forbids women to appear for others, and the reason for this prohibition is to prevent them from interfering in the cases of others, contrary to what is becoming the modesty of their sex, and in order that women may not perform duties which belong to men. The origin of this restriction was derived from the case of a certain Carfania, an extremely shameless woman, whose effrontery and annoyance of the magistrate gave rise to this Edict. (Scott, 3:4)

The French editors of the critical edition point out (17, line 33 n.; 79, line 9 n.) that several texts contemporary with Agrippa use the name Calpurnia rather than Afrania, an error corrected by Charondas le Caron in his commentary on one of these texts in 1603. Agrippa was doubtless working from one of these erroneous sources. Scott, in his translation, uses neither form but yet another alternative. Christine de Pizan alludes to this case but confesses that she does not know the name of the woman (*Book of the City of Ladies*, 31).

178. Rodríguez argues similarly to Agrippa, that men prevent women from studying out of jealousy that women might surpass them.

179. See n. 143.

180. This same example appears in Agrippa's *Of the Vanitie and Uncertaintie of Artes and Sciences*, 23. But I have not found any source for these names.

maternal language? For no other reason have Plato and Quintilian recom-
mended applying so much care to the choice of a good nurse for infants than
that the language and speech of the infant may be correctly and judiciously
formed.[181]

Are not the poets with their trifles and fables and the dialecticians with
their verbal disputes now surpassed by women? There exists nowhere an orator more persuasive than the least of prostitutes. What arithmetician, by cal-
culating wrongly, can deceive a woman paying a debt? What musician can
equal her in singing and charm of voice? Are not philosophers, mathemati-
cians, and astrologers quite often inferior to country women in their predic-
tions and diagnoses? Is it not often the case that a small, aging midwife
outstrips a doctor? Socrates himself, the wisest of all men if one trusts the
testimony of Apollo, did not find it unworthy of him, although he was already very old, still to be learning something from a woman, Aspasia; no
more than the theologian Apollos blushed to be instructed by Priscilla.[182]

If one inquires also about their wisdom, one finds examples in Opis, who
was placed in the number of goddesses, in Plotina, the wife of Trajan, in Amalasuntha, the queen of the Ostrogoths, in Aemilia, the wife of Scipio.[183] In

---

181. Plato, *Republic*, 5.460c–d says that women should be appointed to supervise the nursing of
the guardians' children; the purpose, however, is not so that speech may be correctly formed but
so that mothers will not recognize their own children. *Laws*, 6.766a–b speaks of appointing the
best citizens as teachers of the young (children, not infants) but invokes as the reason not so that
speech may be correctly formed but so that the children will not turn into savages—which
would happen without a proper education. Quintilian, 1.1.4–5, is more to Agrippa's point:
"Above all see that the child's nurse speaks correctly. The ideal, according to Chrysippus, would
be that she should be a philosopher: failing that he desired that the best should be chosen as far
as possible. No doubt the most important point is that they should be of good character: but
they should speak correctly as well. It is the nurse that the child first hears, and her words that he
will first attempt to imitate" (LCL, 1:21).

182. On Aspasia see n. 173. On Apollos being instructed by Priscilla see Acts 18:24–28 and
above, nn. 161 and 170 and related texts.

183. On Opis see Virgil, *Aeneid*, 11.836–67.

Pliny eulogizes Plotina in his *Panegyric of Trajan*, 83.5–8. In the chapter "Hadrian" in the *Augustan
History* she is mentioned twice in significant contexts: she is instrumental in getting Hadrian
adopted by Trajan (4.10), and Hadrian builds a basilica of marvelous workmanship in her honor
(12.2–4). See LCL, *Scriptores historiae Augustae*, 1:29, 37.

Amalasuntha was the daughter of Theodoric, king of the Ostrogoths (d. 526). "From Theodoric's death the years of his system were numbered, but it outlived him owing to the influence
of his widowed daughter, Amalasuntha, whom he had left regent for her young son, Athalaric
(526–534). She was an able woman, bred in Roman culture and heir to her father's ideas, and she
fought an unequal battle with persistence and little scruple. Although she retained the government, the leading Goths soon removed Athalaric from her tuition, and bred him a prematurely
dissolute barbarian. She meanwhile sought the friendship of the Emperor Justinian, whose
hopes for the reconquest of Italy began to grow." And: "The regent Amalasuntha, unpopular for

addition there is the wise Deborah, wife of Lappidoth who, we read in the book of Judges [4–5], served for some time as judge over the people of Israel, who came to her for judgment in all matters. It was she who, after the refusal of Barak to fight against the enemy, was chosen leader of the army of Israel and killed and put to flight its enemies, obtaining the victory. Still further, one reads in the book of Kings that Queen Athalia was sovereign for seven years in Jerusalem.[184]

Semiramis, after the death of King Ninus, governed the people for forty years.[185] All the Candacian queens of Ethiopia, who are mentioned in the Acts of the Apostles, were very wise and powerful sovereigns; Josephus, that trustworthy historian of antiquity, tells some astonishing stories about them.[186] Add to this list Nicaula, queen of Sheba, who came from far away to hear the wisdom of Solomon and who, according to the testimony of the Lord, was going to condemn all the men of Jerusalem.[187] There was also a

---

her pro-Roman ways, was already thinking of refuge in the East when the young Athalaric died (October 534). To keep the throne she married . . . her cousin Theodahad, a miserable specimen of a Romanized Goth, an unreliable coward of literary pretensions. He speedily imprisoned and then murdered the queen in the teeth of her patron Justinian's remonstrances" (Previté-Orton, *Shorter Cambridge Medieval History*, 1:140, 190).

Aemilia knew but remained silent about her husband's infidelity and, after his death, freed the maidservant with whom he had had a liaison and married her to a free man (Valerius Maximus, 6.7.1). See also Boccaccio, *Concerning Famous Women*, chap. 72.

184. Barak did not refuse to fight, he refused to fight unless Deborah accompanied him; she agreed to do so. See Judg. 4:6–15.

In 2 Kings 11 Queen Athalia is presented as a murderer of the rightful ruling family and a worshiper of Baal rather than Yahweh; 2 Kings 11:3 states that the rightful ruler, a child Athaliah had failed to murder, was hidden for six years while she reigned. See also 2 Chron. 22:10–12.

185. Ninus, builder of Nineveh and founder of the Assyrian monarchy (3d millennium BCE), according to the account of Diodorus Siculus, became enamored of Semiramis, wife of one of his officers, and, after threatening to take her from her husband, married her when her husband killed himself in response to the king's threat. Diodorus implies that he reigned only a short time and that Semiramis then took over and extended the Assyrian Empire into North Africa (Egypt, Libya, Ethiopia) and attempted (unsuccessfully) to take India. Hence, the deeds of her husband are attributed to her. Her great feats of building are also described. She did not die but turned the rule over to her son Ninyas and simply disappeared (Diodorus Siculus, 2.4–19). In 2.20 Diodorus tells another story about her, according to which Semiramis was granted rule for five days, during which she had her husband seized and put in prison, reigning thereafter many years and accomplishing many great deeds. In his *Of the Vanitie and Uncertaintie of Artes and Sciences*, 280, Agrippa cites this last story of Diodorus, embellishing it with more lurid details about Semiramis drawn from Boccaccio's largely negative account of her in *Concerning Famous Women*, chap. 2. Not only is all that muted here, but Agrippa's account emphasizes two items stressed by Christine de Pizan in her *Book of the City of Ladies*, 38–40: her long reign (as here) and her conquering the whole world (see below, n. 191).

186. See Acts 8:27ff.; Josephus, *Jewish Antiquities*, 8.165ff., essentially repeats 1 Kings 10.

187. On her coming far to hear the wisdom of Solomon see 1 Kings 10:1–10; 2 Chron. 9:1–9.

very shrewd woman of Tekoa, who snared King David by her questioning, taught him through a riddle, and softened him by the example of God.[188] And not to be overlooked are Abigail and Bathsheba: the first freed her husband from the wrath of David and became after his death the queen and wife of David; the other, mother of Solomon, through her prudence, obtained the kingdom for her son.[189]

In the matter of inventions we may cite as examples Isis, Minerva, Nicostrata;[190] in the foundation of empires and of cities, Semiramis, who held the kingdom of the entire world, Dido, and the Amazons;[191] in fighting wars, Thamyris, queen of the Massagetae (Scythians) who conquered Cyrus the king of Persia, the Volscian Camilla, the Bohemian Valasca, both power-

---

On the testimony of the Lord see Matt. 12:42; Luke 11:31. See also Boccaccio, *Concerning Famous Women*, chap. 41.

188. 2 Sam. 14:4–20.

189. See nn. 48 and 142 (on Abigail) and 49 and 138 (on Bathsheba) and related texts.

190. Isis was an Egyptian goddess who became queen of heaven in the Hellenistic world. One list of her praises begins: "I am Isis, the mistress of every land, and I was taught by Hermes, and with Hermes I devised letters, both the sacred [hieroglyphs] and the demotic, that all things might not be written with the same [letters]." See *Hellenistic Religions: The Age of Syncretism*, ed. Frederick C. Grant (New York, 1953), 131–33. See also Boccaccio, *Concerning Famous Women*, chap. 8, who attributes to her, among other things, the invention of "letters suitable for the language of the men of that country. She then showed how to place them together to those who were ready to learn" (19).

Minerva is the Greek goddess Athena, patroness of the city of Athens and of arts and crafts; she is also a goddess of war. She ultimately became personified as the goddess of wisdom, a tendency already visible in Hesiod (*Theogony*, 886ff.). See Boccaccio, *Concerning Famous Women*, chap. 6, where she is credited with discovery of the art of working in wool, invention of the cart and iron weapons, covering the body with armor, numbers, and the flute or shepherd's pipes. Christine de Pizan repeats all these inventions (which led to Minerva's reputation for wisdom) in *Book of the City of Ladies*, 73–74. Rodríguez, in reason 20 for the superiority of women, simply credits her with founding the sciences (230).

Nicostrata (also called Carmenta) was credited by the Romans with the invention of the alphabet. See Livy, 1.7; Virgil, *Aeneid*, 8.338. See also Boccaccio, *Concerning Famous Women*, chap. 25. Christine de Pizan also credits her with being the first to institute laws in Rome—not mentioned by Boccaccio (*Book of the City of Ladies*, 71). Rodríguez mentions her as the founder of the Latin language in reason 20 for the superiority of women (230).

191. On Semiramis, see n. 185.

Boccaccio tells the story of Dido's founding of Carthage in the latter part of his account, *Concerning Famous Women*, chap. 40.

In Greek mythology the Amazons were a society of female warriors located at the edges of the known world. They appear early in the Greek tradition (*Iliad*, 3.189; 6.186) and continued to fascinate the Hellenistic world. Plutarch, for example, vividly recounts several versions of their relation to Heracles/Hercules (Plutarch, *Theseus*, 26). In *Of the Vanitie and Uncertaintie of Artes and Sciences*, Agrippa writes about the Amazons: "I will also pass over the governance of women gotten by the murders of men, as the Histories do record of the *Amazons*" (282–83, spelling modernized).

ful queens,[192] as well as the Pandea of India, the Amazons, the Candaces, the women of Lemnos, of Phocis, of Chios, and of Persia.[193]

We read of many other illustrious women whose marvelous courage saved their entire nation from a desperate situation. Among them is Judith, whom St. Jerome praises in these words: "See in the widow Judith an example of chastity, celebrate her with triumphal praise and continual eulogies."[194]

192. On Thamyris see Valerius Maximus, 9.10.Ext. 1; and Boccaccio, *Concerning Famous Women*, chap. 47. See also Herodotus, 1.206–16.

On Camilla see n. 146.

Jungmayr (356 n. 227) says about Valasca that she was the ringleader of a female government in the eighth century CE; together with her husband she took power after the death of the Bohemian princess Libussa. She controlled the greater part of Bohemia and even enlarged its boundaries. She insisted on being trained in warfare. Her tyrannical government lasted seven years, after which the people rose in revolt. Jungmayr cites Johann Heinrich Zedler, *Grosses voll-standiges Universal-Lexicon, aller Wissenschaften und Künste*, 64 vols. (Halle, 1732–50), 46:140.

193. The Pandae were a people in India who came to be ruled by women, to whom a sister of Hercules, Pandaea or Pandea, bears evidence; for she subsequently ruled over one of the greatest kingdoms of these people (Jungmayr, 356 n. 228, citing Zedler, ibid., 26:503).

Candaces is a title given to Ethiopian queens, as Agrippa has said slightly earlier in the text. One of them was baptized by Philip. See Acts 8:26–38.

The Lemniadae are women from the island of Lemnos who, together with women from Thrace, put all the males on the entire island to death and elected Hypsipyle to rule over them. See Statius, *Thebiad*, 5.29; Ovid, *Heroides*, 6.

The Phocians, threatened by the Thessalians with death for Phocian men and slavery for the women and children, voted not only to fight but to gather the women and children together and burn them if they found themselves losing the battle. Daiphantus persuaded the men not to impose this on the women without their consent; the women subsequently met and approved the vote—it is also said that the children did the same (Plutarch, *Bravery of Women*, 244).

Plutarch tells two stories about the women of Chios. In the first, when the Chians agreed to lay down their arms and leave the city with one cloak, their women chided them to claim that their spears were their cloaks and their shields their shirts. The Chians did so, frightening their enemies, who left. Thus, they were taught courage by their women and were saved. In the second story, the city was being besieged by Philip (201 BCE) who said that slaves who deserted to him would be set free and given in marriage to the wives of their masters, whereupon both slaves and women of Chios joined together to fight with the men of the city so vigorously that Philip was repulsed; not one slave defected to him (*The Bravery of Women*, 244–45).

Of the women of Persia Plutarch writes that when Cyrus and his Persian army were fleeing home after having been defeated in battle, they were met as they arrived at the city by their women, who, lifting their skirts, chided them with being unable to slink back whence they had come forth. Mortified by this sight and the words, the Persians rallied, fought, and won, leading to a custom later referred to by Agrippa (Plutarch, *Bravery of Women*, 246).

194. Jud. 7–15, and above, nn. 53, 122, and 158 and related texts. Here again Agrippa is reversing a common topos used against women: that they have led kings and nations to destruction. Marbot of Rennes (1035–1123) so argued in his *De meretrice* (*PL*, 171:1,693). Christine de Pizan had argued as Agrippa does here, using the same examples, in her *Book of the City of Ladies* (143ff.).

The statement from Jerome may be found in the prologue to the book of Judith in the Vulgate (Stuttgart, 1983), 691 (see Jungmayr, 356 n. 230). See also Jerome, *Letters*, 54.16. Jerome wrote: "In the book of Judith—if any one is of opinion that it should be received as canonical—

God has given her as an example not only to women but also to men and in order to recompense her chastity gave her such virtue that she conquered one who had never been conquered and surpassed one who was unsurpassable.

We read also that a strong wise woman summoned Joab, put in his hands the head of Sheba, the enemy of David, in order to save the city of Abel, mother city of all other cities of Israel.[195] And a woman, throwing a fragment of a millstone, struck Abimelech's head and shattered his skull, thus completing the revenge of God on Abimelech, who had wronged his father before the Lord by killing his seventy brothers on one rock.[196] Esther, the wife of king Ahasuerus, not only freed her people from a disgraceful death but obtained for them, in addition, the greatest honors.[197] When Rome was besieged by the Volscians commanded by Gnaeus Marcius Coriolanus and the men were not able to defend their city by arms, Veturia, an elderly woman and the mother of Coriolanus, saved the city by scolding her son.[198] When the Rhodians were attacking her, Artemisia both stripped them of their fleet and made herself mistress of their island, building in the city of Rhodes a statue in order to brand a permanent mark of shame on it.[199]

Who in our day will be able to praise enough the noble young girl [Joan of Arc]? Though of humble origin, she took up arms like an Amazon in 1428 when the English occupied France, placed herself at the head of the army, and fought so vigorously and successfully that she conquered the English in numerous battles and restored to the king of France a kingdom he had already lost. At Genabum (that is to say Orleans), on the bridge over the Loire, a statue dedicated to the Maid has been erected to commemorate her exploits.[200]

---

we read of a widow wasted with fasting and wearing the sombre garb of a mourner, whose outward squalor indicated not so much the regret which she felt for her dead husband as the temper [i.e., penitence] in which she looked forward to the coming of the Bridegroom. I see her hand armed with the sword and stained with blood. I recognize the head of Holofernes which she has carried away from the camp of the enemy. Here a woman vanquishes men, and chastity beheads lust. Quickly changing her garb, she puts on once more in the hour of victory her own mean dress finer than all the splendors of the world" (*NPNF*, ser. 2, 6:108).

195. 2 Sam. 20:14–22.

196. Judg. 9, especially 9:1–6, 50–57.

197. Esther 8–9; see also above, nn. 52 and 158 and related texts.

198. See Livy, 2.40.1; Plutarch, *Coriolanus*, 34; and Boccaccio, *Concerning Famous Women*, chap. 53.

199. On Artemisia, see n. 142.

200. Christine de Pizan, a contemporary of Joan of Arc (1412–31), composed a poem praising her, the only work praising Joan written during her lifetime, and the very last of Christine's

From the histories of Greeks, Latins, and barbarians, ancient as well as modern, I could still recount innumerable exceptional women, but in order not to extend this work beyond measure, I have striven to remain silent. Plutarch, Valerius Maximus, Boccaccio, and several others have written their stories.[201] This is why the things that I have cited to the glory of women are less numerous than all those that I have passed in silence, for I am not ambitious enough to pretend to be able to enclose in so small a treatise the infinite excellences and virtues of women. Who, indeed, would be equal to taking a census of the infinite praises women merit, they who are at the origin of all our being, who assure the conservation of the human race (which would, without them, be lost in a very short time), they on whom depend every family and every state?

The founder of Rome was not ignorant of this. As women were lacking, he did not hesitate to undertake a war without mercy against the Sabines, whose daughters he had abducted, for he knew that his kingdom would perish in a short time if there were no women there. When the Capitoline had been captured by the Sabines, and while the bloody battle raged in the middle of the forum, the fighting stopped when the women ran between the two battle lines. Finally they made peace and concluded a treaty, which marked the beginning of a perpetual friendship. It is for this reason that Romulus gave women's names to the curias[202] and that the Romans agreed to a stipulation in the official registers that the women would neither have to grind nor prepare food. Moreover, wife and husband were prohibited from accepting gifts from one another, so that they would know they had all interests in common. Hence, finally, the custom appeared that those taking a bride bid her say: "Where you are, I am,"[203] signifying by that: "Where you are lord, I am lady," "where you are master, I am mistress."

writings (Christine de Pizan, *Ditié de Jehanne d'Arc*, ed. Angus J. Kennedy and Kenneth Varty. Medium Aevum Monographs, n.s. 9 [Oxford, 1977]; see also Charity Cannon Willard, *Christine de Pizan: Her Life and Works* (New York, 1984), passim and 204–7 for a discussion of the poem. Martin Le Franc, *Le Champion des dames*, closes his work with a paean to Joan and the Virgin Mary (see the introduction). For a recent reinterpretation of Joan see Anne Llewellyn Barstow, *Joan of Arc: Heretic, Mystic, Shaman* (Lewiston, N.Y., 1986) and sources cited.

201. On Plutarch and Boccaccio see the introduction, n. 1, and related text. On Valerius Maximus see the translation, n. 69.

202. See Livy, 1.9–13. In 1.13 Livy states that Romulus divided the Roman population into thirty wards (curias), giving to them the names of the women who had thus intervened. Livy also states here that the Romans, as a gesture to the Sabines, called themselves Quirites after the Sabine town of Cures.

203. *Digest*, 24.1.1: "In accordance with the custom adopted by us, gifts between husband and

After the expulsion of the kings the legions of the Volscians led by Marcius Coriolanus established their camp five miles [from Rome]; they were turned back [through the intervention of] the women, and, in recompense for this benefit, a magnificent temple was dedicated to the Fortune of women.[204] Even further, great honors and tokens of esteem were conferred on them by a decree of the Senate, such as the privilege of walking on the high side of the street, and men rising to render homage to them and ceding their place to them. They were permitted to wear purple garments with golden fringes, even ornaments of precious stones, earrings, rings, and necklaces.

The later emperors stipulated that if a law were promulgated prohibiting the wearing of particular garments or jewelry, women were not included under it.[205] In addition they were granted succession to inheritances and to rights over property.[206] Laws also permitted the funerals of women to be celebrated like those of illustrious men with eulogies delivered in public, in commemoration of the time when a present was to be sent to Apollo at Del-

---

wife are not valid. This rule has been adopted to prevent married persons from despoiling themselves through mutual affection, by setting no limits to their generosity, but being too profuse toward one another through the facility afforded them to do so" (Scott, 5:302).

The marriage ceremony was not established in Roman law but in custom; hence, the phrase in Agrippa's text does not appear in the law code. See S. M. Treggiari, *Roman Marriage: Iusti Coniuges from the Time of Cicero to the Time of Ulpian* (New York, 1991).

204. On Coriolanus see Livy, 2.40.1. On the temple dedicated to the women see Plutarch, *Caius Marcius Coriolanus*, 37. Plutarch recounts that when the Volscians departed all the temples were thrown open. The women were extolled for saving the city, and the Senate offered them any reward they wished. They asked only for the erection of a temple to the goddess Fortune, the expense of which they would bear themselves if the temple would be kept up at public expense. This was agreed to, and the women were extolled for their public spirit (*Lives*, 4.211).

205. See *Code*, 11.11, Nulli licere in frenis ("No One Shall be Permitted to Adorn"; Scott 15:178): "no private person shall be permitted to make anything out of gold and jewels, which is reserved for Imperial use and adornment (with the exception of ornaments usually worn by women, and the rings of both sexes)."

206. Women could inherit but, according to the Lex Voconia of 168 BCE, could not be the primary beneficiary if the family to which they belonged was among the most wealthy according to the census. The point seems to have been to bar women, not from being rich, but from being rich and independent or to prevent the bulk of the family fortune from passing out of the male line. Even this rule died out in the early Empire because the census was no longer in use. The rule never applied in cases where there was no will. In the latter cases a guardian was sometimes appointed from the paternal family to give his authorization for more important transactions or acts such as the manumission of slaves. But even this was not a universal practice. Women were not named as heirs in the Law of the Twelve Tables, which means they were not considered relatives. The practice of naming them heirs came later, and the Lex Voconia was perhaps a check on this. See W. W. Buckland, *A Text-Book of Roman Law from Augustus to Justinian*, 2d ed. (Cambridge, 1932), 290–91.

phi in conformity with a vow of Camillus, and there was not enough gold in the city, the women spontaneously contributed their jewelry.²⁰⁷ In the course of the war of Cyrus against Astyages the Persian army was already in flight when, consumed by the reproaches of the women, it returned to the struggle and gave the women a remarkable victory. For this reason Cyrus stipulated in a law that every time the Persian kings entered the city, they should pay to each woman a crown of gold. Alexander, who entered the city twice, also twice paid this impost. Alexander even doubled the sum for pregnant women.²⁰⁸ Thus, the ancient kings of Persia, as the Romans (and the latter from the beginning of Rome itself and of its sovereignty), have always bestowed upon women all sorts of honors.

They were no less respected by the emperors themselves. The emperor Justinian was of the opinion that in making laws, his wife ought to be consulted and involved.²⁰⁹ And in another place a law said: "A wife shares in the honor given to her husband to the point of feeling his renown, and she is elevated in rank as high as her spouse." Thus, the wife of an emperor is called empress, that of a king queen, that of a prince princess, and she is illustrious no matter what the circumstances of her birth.²¹⁰ Ulpian says: "The prince, that is to say the emperor, is not subject to the laws; although the Augusta, who is the spouse of the emperor, is subject to the laws, the prince nonetheless bestows on her the same privileges he has himself."²¹¹

This [bestowal of privilege] is what permits noble women to be judges

207. Plutarch, *Camillus*, 8.2–3. Camillus had vowed to send one-tenth of the booty from his victory at Veii to Delphi. He did not do so—presumably he forgot his vow—and the vow had to be filled later when the soldiers had spent much of what they had won at Veii. The women of Rome contributed gold ornaments weighing eight talents and were rewarded as Agrippa relates.

208. Plutarch, *Bravery of Women*, 246a–b.

209. See *Novels*, 8: Ut magistratus sine ulla donatione fiant ("Judges Shall Not Obtain Their Offices by Purchase"), cap. 1, "Concerning Magistrates Who Should Be Created without Expense": "Having reflected upon all these matters, and discussed them with Our Most August Consort, whom God has given Us . . . " (Scott, 16:53).

210. *Code*, 5.4, De nuptiis ("Concerning Marriage"), 29; *Novels*, 105, De consultibus ("Concerning Consuls"), cap. 2: "Concerning the Wife and the Mother of the Consul": "If the Consul has a wife, we regulate her expenses also, for it is proper for her to share the distinction of her husband. . . . No other woman than the wife and the mother of the Consul shall be distinguished in this manner; for the reason that wives, in accordance with law, share the distinction of their husbands, and mothers also enjoy it if the Consul so desires" (Scott, 17:17–18).

211. See *Digest*, 1.3, De legibus ("Concerning Statutes, Decrees of the Senate, and Long Established Customs"). The citation from Ulpian is from book 13, "On the Lex Julia et Papia": "The Emperor is free from the operation of the law, and though the Empress is undoubtedly subject to it, still, the Emperors generally confer upon her the same privileges which they themselves enjoy" (Scott, 2:225).

and arbitrators,[212] to have power to invest or be invested with a fief, and to decide a matter of law among their vassals.[213] For the same reason a woman, as a man, can have slaves of her own,[214] she can render justice even among foreigners,[215] and she can give her name to her family, so that her sons receive the name of their mother rather than of their father.[216] They also have great privileges in what concerns their dowry, which are explained at various points in the body of the law.[217] It is even stipulated there that a respectable woman of good reputation should not be incarcerated for civil debts; on the contrary, the judge who puts her in prison is punished with the loss of his

212. Gregory IX, *Decretals*, 1.43, De arbitris, cap. 4, Dilecti, lines 13–15: "Quamvis autem secundum regulam juris civilis foeminae a publicis officiis sint remotae" (Moreover, according to the rule of civil law women are not allowed to hold public offices). The same view is elaborated in the *Digest*, 50.17.2: "Women are excluded from all civil or public employments; therefore they cannot be judges, or perform the duties of magistrates, or bring suits in court, or become sureties for others, or act as attorneys" (Scott, 11:297). These texts thus say the opposite of what Agrippa is contending.

213. "Renaissance jurists also consider the succession of women to fiefs. There are such things as 'feuda mulierum'; some abbesses can hold fiefs. But in general ('regulariter') women are excluded from succession to them" (Maclean, 74, and sources cited, nn. 28 and 29). Women who did hold fiefs could, of course, decide a matter of law among their vassals. And this seems to be Agrippa's point.

214. *Digest*, 15.1, De peculio ("Concerning the Action on the Peculium"), 3, par. 2: "It is of little importance whether a slave belongs to a man or a woman, for a woman can also be sued in an action on the peculium" (Scott, 4:236). "Peculium" is a sum set aside by a master for a slave.

215. I have found no instances in Roman law stipulating that a woman can render such judgments. But nothing prevents them, since Roman law does not regulate legal relations among foreigners, only among citizens.

216. In the later Republican period Roman law provided that children could inherit from their mother, but I am unaware of any statement in the *Corpus iuris civilis* stipulating that children could take the name of the cognatic (maternal) line rather than that of the agnatic (paternal) line. In the Middle Ages, however, some men married women whose status was markedly higher than theirs and in whose families there were no male heirs. In such cases the husband might have taken the wife's family name. Agrippa may well have had this in mind.

217. *Digest*, 23.3–5, stipulates privileges and legal judgments associated with dowries. *Digest*, 3.1.1 and 3.1.2, essentially make Agrippa's point: 3.1.1 (Paul): "The right of the dowry is perpetual, and, in accordance with the desire of the party who bestows it, the contract is made with the understanding that the dowry will always remain in the hands of the husband." And 3.1.2: "It is to the interest of the state that women should have their dowries preserved, in order that they may marry again" (Scott, 5:261).

The question of dowries is also addressed at other points in the law, as Agrippa states. One of these is *Code*, 6.20, De collationibus ("Concerning Hotchpot"), 3: "A clause included in a dotal instrument providing that the woman shall be contented with the dowry given at marriage, and shall have no right to the estate of her father, is disapproved by the law, and the daughter cannot for this reason be prevented from succeeding to the estate of her father if he dies without a will. She must, however, account to her brothers, who remained under the control of their father, for the dowry which she received" (231 CE) (Scott, 13:314).

life.[218] If she is suspected of some offense, she is thrust into a monastery or given over to women to be incarcerated, because, as the law attests, the woman is of a better condition than the man, and also because, when the offenses are similar, the man is more guilty than the woman. Thus, the man convicted of adultery is punished with death, while the female adulterer is thrust into a convent.[219] Azo has assembled more privileges of women in his summary [of the section of the *Digest*] "On the Velleian Decree of the Senate,"[220] and the Investigator has assembled those "On Renunciations."[221]

218. *Code*, 1.48: De officio diversorum judicum ("Concerning the Duties of Various Judges"), 1: "Let no judge think that an officer may be sent with an order to a house in which the mother of a family resides, for the purpose of publicly arresting her, as it is certain that the debts of one who, on account of her sex, remains at home, can be paid by the sale of her house, or any of her property; because if any one should, after this, believe that the mother of a family can be publicly arrested, he shall be reckoned among the greatest of criminals, and be condemned to the penalty of death, without any indulgence whatever" (316 CE) (Scott, 12:151).

219. *Code*, 9.4, De custodia rerum ("Concerning the Custody of Accused Persons"), 3: "If the crime of which she is accused is of the most serious description, she shall be placed in a monastery, or a nunnery, or delivered to certain women by whom she shall be guarded" (Scott, 14:364). *Novels*, 134.10, prescribes death to the man, confinement in a monastery to the woman (fourth cent. CE).

In *Novels*, 134.9, it is stated that the reason for not putting a woman in prison guarded by men is that her chastity may be violated.

Gratian, *Decretum*, 2, causa 32, quaestio 6, canon 4: "Indignantur mariti si audiant adulteros viros pendere similes adulteris feminis penas: cum tanto gravius eos puniri oportuerit, quanto magis ad eos pertinet et virtuti vincere et exemplo regere feminas" (Husbands are indignant if they hear that adulterous men are given the same penalties as adulterous women, because they ought to be punished more severely inasmuch as it falls much more to them to become masters by virtue and to rule their wives by example).

See also, *Code*, 9.9, Ad legem Juliam de adulteriis et stupro ("On the Lex Julia Relating to Adultery and Fornication"), 30. It is said here, among other things, that in order to prevent discord only immediate family members may accuse a woman of adultery, and that if a husband catches his wife in the act of adultery "he can kill her without any risk to himself" (Scott, 15:15ff.).

220. Azo (or Azzo, d. 1230) was a professor of law at Bologna and the most famous of the glossators who flourished during the twelfth and thirteenth centuries. His greatest work was his *Summa* of the *Institutes* and *Code*, a work regarded as essential as the text of the *Corpus iuris civilis* itself; a knowledge of it was necessary to anyone who wished to enter the guild of judges.

The resolution "On the Velleian Decree of the Senate" is the subject of the *Digest*, 16.1. The Velleian decree stipulates that a woman cannot become surety for anyone; she is deprived of civil office and so of the power to perform an act in which her services would be employed and her property at risk. The decree adds that it is just to come to the relief of the woman in this way to protect her if she has been made liable (e.g., for a debt) by a man. There is much commentary on this decree in the *Digest*.

Code, 4.29, par. 2, states: "the exception of the Decree of the Senate is only granted to a woman where she herself owes nothing as principal, but has become surety to a creditor for another debtor" (213 CE) (Scott, 13:63). The *Code* has additional commentary on the law (Scott, 13:63–70). See J. A. Crook, "Feminine Inadequacy and the Senatusconsultum Velleianum," in Beryl Rawson, ed., *The Family in Ancient Rome* (Ithaca, N.Y., 1986), 83–91.

221. The Investigator is William Durand (1237–96), author of *Speculum judiciale*, first published in 1271 but also numerous times thereafter.

Of ancient legislators and founders of states, Lycurgus and Plato, men of weight because of their wisdom and absolutely competent because of their knowledge, knowing by the secrets of philosophy that women are not inferior to men either in the quality of their minds or in their physical strength, or in the dignity of their nature, but that they are as adroit in all these respects, decreed that women should exercise with men in wrestling and gymnastics, even in all that touches military training—the bow, sling, rock throwing, shooting arrows, jousting with arms on horse or on foot, knowing how to set up camp and a line of battle, directing the army; to be brief, men and women are assigned absolutely identical exercises.[222]

Let us read trustworthy historians from antiquity. We shall discover in them that in Getulia, among the Bactrians, and in Galletia, it was the practice for men to devote themselves to leisure while the women cultivated the fields, constructed buildings, carried on commerce, rode horses, fought, and did other things that in our day men normally do. Among the Cantabrians [in Spain] men gave a dowry to the women, brothers were given in marriage by their sisters, daughters were the designated heirs. Among the Scythians, the Thracians, and the Gauls, duties were common to men and to women.[223] When there were deliberations about war and peace, women were brought in for the discussions and the decision. The proof of this is the treaty struck between Hannibal and the Celts, on the following terms: "If anyone of the Celts complains of having suffered an injustice at the hands of anyone of the Carthaginians, the Carthaginian magistrates or the generals who are in Spain will be judges of the dispute. If anyone of the Carthaginians has suffered an injustice at the hand of anyone of the Celts, the women of the Celts shall pass judgment on the matter."[224]

WHY WOMEN ARE NOT RECOGNIZED TODAY

But since the excessive tyranny of men prevails over divine right and natural laws, the freedom that was once accorded to women is in our day obstructed

222. On Lycurgus see Plutarch, *Life of Lycurgus*, 14.3–4. Lycurgus ordered women to exercise by wrestling, throwing darts, etc., so that the children they carried while pregnant might be healthier and they might better endure the pains of childbirth. On Plato see *Republic*, 5.456a–b. Plato, however, says that the only difference between men and women is that women are weaker than men.

223. Getulia or Gaetulia is Libya (see Jungmayr, 358 n. 257, citing Zedler, *Grosses vollstandiges Universal-Lexicon*, 10:55f.), part of Bactria, a Persian province (see Jungmayr, 358 n. 257, citing Zedler, *Grosses vollstandiges Universal-Lexicon*, 3:75f.). Galletia is Galatia in Asia Minor; Paul established a Christian church in that region. The Cantabrians are a tribe in Spain. I have located no sources for Agrippa's assertions about these groups or for those about the Scythians, Thracians, and Gauls.

224. Plutarch, *Bravery of Women*, 246C.

by unjust laws, suppressed by custom and usage, reduced to nothing by education. For as soon as she is born a woman is confined in idleness at home from her earliest years, and, as if incapable of functions more important, she has no other prospect than needle and thread. Further, when she has reached the age of puberty, she is delivered over to the jealous power of a husband, or she is enclosed forever in a workhouse for religious. She is forbidden by law to hold public office;[225] even the most shrewd among them are not permitted to bring a suit in court.

In addition women are excluded from the court, from judgments, from adoption, from intercession, from administration, from the right of trusteeship, from guardianship, from matters of inheritance, and from criminal trials.[226] They are excluded also from preaching the word of God,[227] in contradiction to Scripture where the Holy Spirit, by the mouth of Joel, has promised them: "Your daughters also will prophesy." In this spirit women taught publicly in the time of the Apostles, as we know from Anna, wife of Simeon, from the daughters of Philip, and from Priscilla, wife of Aquila.[228] But our modern legislators are of such bad faith that they have made null and void the commandment of God, they have decreed according to their own traditions that women, however otherwise naturally eminent and of remarkable nobility, are inferior in status to all men.[229] And so these laws compel women to submit to men, as conquered before conquerors, and that without reason or necessity natural or divine, but under the pressure of custom, education, chance, or some occasion favorable to tyranny.

There are, in addition, those who have assumed authority in religion and exercised it over women, basing their tyranny on Holy Scripture; the curse

225. The sentiments expressed here are very similar to those expressed by Maria Equicola in his *De mulieribus* (a5v–a6r), written at Mantua around 1501. See the introduction.

226. *Digest*, 50.17, De diversis regulis juris antiqui ("Concerning Different Rules of Ancient Law"), 2: "Women are excluded from all civic or public employments; therefore they cannot be judges or perform the duties of magistrates, or bring suits in court, or become sureties for others, or act as attorneys" (Scott, 11:297).

227. Gratian, *Decretum*, 2, causa 33, quaestio 5, canon 17: "Mulierem constat subjectam dominio viri esse et nullam auctoritatem habere, nec docere potest, nec testis esse, neque fidem dare, nec judicare" (It is agreed that a woman is subject to the dominion of a man and that she has no authority; she cannot teach or be a witness, she cannot swear an oath or be a judge). See also *Digest*, 3.1, De postulando ("Concerning the Right Application to the Court"), 6.

228. On the daughters of Joel see Joel 2:28; see also Acts 2:17. On the wife of Simeon see Luke 2:36–38, and above, n. 161 and related text. On the daughters of Philip see Acts 21:9 and above, nn. 161 and 170 and related texts. On Priscilla see Acts 18:24–28 and above, text related to nn. 164 and 182.

229. *Digest*, 1.5, De statu hominum ("Concerning the Condition of Man") 9: "In many parts of our law the condition of women is worse than that of men" (Scott, 2:229).

on Eve is continually in their mouth: "You will be under the power of your husband and he will rule over you." If it is responded to them that Christ has put an end to this curse, they will make the same rebuttal again, from the words of Peter, adding to them also those of Paul: "Women are to be subject to men. Women are to be silent in Church."[230]

But one who knows the various figures of speech and meanings of Scripture will easily see that these phrases contradict themselves only in appearance. There is in reality an order in the church which places men before women in the ministry, just as the Jews have been placed before the Greeks according to the promise. However, God has a preference for no one, for in Christ there is neither male nor female, but a new creation.[231] Even more, many offenses against women have been allowed to men because of their hardness of heart—for example, divorces, which were in earlier times permitted to the Jews;[232] but such things do no injury to the status of women, since, if their husbands fail in their duty or commit a crime, the women have the power of judgment to the shame of the men. The queen of Sheba herself is going to judge the men of Jerusalem.[233] Therefore those who are justified by faith and have become the sons of Abraham, that is to say, sons of the promise, are in the power of a woman and subject to the command of God, who says to Abraham: "Whatever your wife Sarah says to you, obey her words."[234]

CONCLUDING SUMMARY

Now, to sum up as briefly as possible, I have shown the preeminence of the female sex according to her name, order, place, and material of her creation, and the status superior to man she has received from God. Moreover, I have demonstrated this with respect to religion, nature, and human laws, and [in each case] through diverse authorities, reasons, and examples. However, as numerous as have been my arguments, I have left still more numerous points untreated, because neither personal ambition nor the desire to make the most

---

230. On the husband ruling over his wife see Gen. 3:16. In 1 Pet. 3:1 the writer says that women should be subject to their husbands. Two "Pauline" texts are cited by Agrippa: Col. 3:18 and Ephesians 5:22. These and other texts on this subject are discussed in the introduction.

231. See Rom. 2:9–10; Galatians 3:28; 2 Cor. 5:17.

232. Deut. 24:1ff.

233. Matt. 12:42; Luke 11:31.

234. See Rom. 4:16, 9:8; Galatians 3:9. The quotation is from Gen. 21:12; see also above, nn. 92 and 158 and related texts.

of myself but duty and truth moved me to write. I did not want to appear, if I kept silent, to steal from so devoted a sex—by an impious silence—the praises owed to it (as it were burying the talent entrusted to me).

But if anyone more diligent than I finds some argument I have overlooked that he thinks should be added to this work of mine, I shall believe that I have not been discredited but rather supported by him in the measure to which he will make better this good work of mine through his talent and his learning.[235]

And now, lest this work turn into a huge book, let this be the end of it.

235. Many writers borrowed from and copied Agrippa, and a number of translators also embellished his text. See the introduction, and above, n. 123.

INDEX OF BIBLICAL REFERENCES

GENERAL INDEX